Supporting English Learners
in the Reading Workshop

GRADES K–5

Supporting English Learners in the Reading Workshop

Lindsey Moses

HEINEMANN
Portsmouth, NH

Heinemann
361 Hanover Street
Portsmouth, NH 03801–3912
www.heinemann.com

Offices and agents throughout the world

The author and publisher wish to thank those who have generously given permission to reprint borrowed material:

Figures 1.1, 1.2, Word Work lesson, and Figure 6.3: Adapted from *Comprehension and English Language Learners: 25 Oral Reading Strategies That Cross Proficiency Levels* by Michael F. Opitz with Lindsey Moses. Copyright © 2009 by Michael F. Opitz and Lindsey Moses. Published by Heinemann, Portsmouth, NH. All rights reserved.

Figure 6.1: Text and illustration from *HOUGHTON MIFFLIN LEVELED READER: A Walk in the Woods* by Nora Bingham. Copyright © 2004 by Houghton Mifflin Harcourt. All rights reserved. Reprinted by permission of the publisher, Houghton Mifflin Harcourt Publishing Company.

Cataloging-in-Publication Data is on file at the Library of Congress.
ISBN: 978-0-325-05757-6

Editor: Holly Kim Price
Production: Victoria Merecki
Cover design: Suzanne Heiser
Interior design: Shawn Girsberger
Typesetter: Shawn Girsberger
Manufacturing: Steve Bernier

Printed in the United States of America on acid-free paper
20 19 18 17 16 15   VP   1 2 3 4 5

To my parents,
Mike and Karen Moses,
for being my first teachers and biggest supporters.

Contents

Acknowledgments

I WOULD LIKE TO ACKNOWLEDGE:

My former students, who were the original inspiration to find effective ways to support English learners in the reading workshop.

My former principal, Augie Lopez, who provided the support, encouragement, and space that allowed me to grow as a professional.

The wonderful teachers with whom I have had the privilege to work alongside while sharing my ideas for supporting English learners in the reading workshop. I am extremely grateful for the four outstanding teachers who contributed to this book by sharing their experiences and images of supporting English learners in their classrooms following our work together: Beth Rogers, primary Exceptional Student Education teacher at Pinewood Elementary School in Stuart, Florida; Rachael Pritchard, first-grade teacher at Turnberry Elementary School in Commerce City, Colorado; Amy Fletcher, fourth-grade teacher at White Rock Elementary in Dallas, Texas; and Rachel Busetti Frevert, bilingual special education teacher in Brighton, Colorado. Thank you to Meridith Ogden, first-grade teacher at Cactus View Elementary School in Phoenix, Arizona, for welcoming me into her amazing classroom every week for an entire year.

Michelle Flynn, Cheryl Murphy-Savage, and Heinemann PD staff for opportunities to work with amazing schools and teachers over the last three years. Working in these schools has inspired me and made this book possible.

Holly Kim Price and the amazing staff at Heinemann for their feedback and support to bring this book to fruition.

Mary Lou Fulton Teachers College at Arizona State University for their support of my research and writing for this book.

Michael F. Opitz for his mentorship in writing, teaching, and making a difference in the lives of children.

My parents for modeling a love and respect for education that has never wavered.

My partner and fellow author/educator, Frank Serafini, for his endless support and encouragement. I am so thankful to have a partner who listens to me talk about book ideas on Sunday runs, enjoys educational banter, and challenges my thinking on a daily basis.

Introduction

OVER THE LAST TEN YEARS, I HAVE HAD MANY CONVERSATIONS ABOUT THE BEST ways to support English learners in elementary classroom settings. The discussions began during my first year of teaching, grew throughout my graduate studies in English as a second language and multicultural and bilingual education, deepened during my doctoral work related to culturally and linguistically diverse education and reading, and continue to evolve as I now work with preservice and practicing teachers in a university setting and in the field as a professional developer. My personal experiences, studies, and work with teachers and children shaped my vision about ways to support English learners through meaningful and rigorous instruction with a reading workshop model approach.

As a second-grade teacher at a bilingual school in Colorado, I provided instruction in English to students who typically spoke English or Spanish as their first language. The majority of my students spoke Spanish as their first language, but approximately one third were monolingual English speakers. We had failed to demonstrate adequate yearly progress (AYP) for three years and experienced the challenges of being required to use a "paced" curriculum with an anthology. As we discussed ways to improve instruction and student learning, my passion for meaningful instruction grounded in a workshop model grew. The importance of thinking, talking, reading, writing, speaking, listening, viewing, and visually representing became obvious as I watched my students engage with literacy in meaningful ways that were missing in our paced curriculum lessons.

Many discussions with colleagues, preservice teachers, and practicing teachers begin with something like, "It sounds great, but I am not sure it would work with (my classroom, my school, my district)." They want to know the practical "how-to" part. That is exactly what I wanted as a new teacher. I needed theoretically sound, research-based instructional ideas to support the students in my classroom. To be honest, I struggled to find the time and energy to investigate the "theoretically sound, research-based" qualifications during my initial attempts at using a workshop model. I needed support for the logistics: getting my classroom workshop ready; ideas for units of study and learning experiences; suggestions for whole-group, small-group, individualized instruction and conferring; and ways to use assessment to drive my instruction. However, I needed these logistics to include the necessary linguistic considerations to support my English learners. The goal of this book is exactly that—to provide support for English learners and teachers getting started in a linguistically diverse workshop setting.

I am a strong proponent of quality bilingual education, and this book in no way suggests moving away from or altering that approach. The purpose of this book is to share effective instructional ideas in settings where teachers may not be able to support students in their first language. For example, I worked with a kindergarten teacher who had eighteen different first languages in her classroom. I have worked with other teachers who have as few as one to as many as a full class of English learners. Like my experience as a teacher, they have to juggle the needs of both bilingual and monolingual students in English in unique classroom settings. The hope is that this book will provide structure, ideas, and support for establishing an effective and supportive reading workshop for English learners.

This book begins with a foundation for the focus of the book, English learners and reading. Chapter One provides a description, with personal vignettes, of English learners. Building on the understanding of English learners, I explain the stages of language proficiency, academic performance of English learners in the United States, and expectations related to standards. Finally, I include my top five research-based tips for supporting English learners in a linguistically diverse reading workshop.

Chapter Two addresses the structure of the reading workshop for English learners and answers common questions about differentiation, schedule possibilities, and standards for English learners. Chapters Three through Seven include the practical instructional ideas for planning and supporting English learners through each component of the reading workshop. These practical chapters include an overview, supporting research, instructional ideas, stories from the classroom, student samples, suggested children's literature, and differentiation and assessment ideas. Each chapter includes examples for primary and intermediate classrooms as well as lessons related to both fiction and informational text. My hope is not that teachers will follow these lessons exactly, but instead that teachers will be encouraged to use this as a platform to create and individualize meaningful instruction for their English learners in their own unique reading workshop setting.

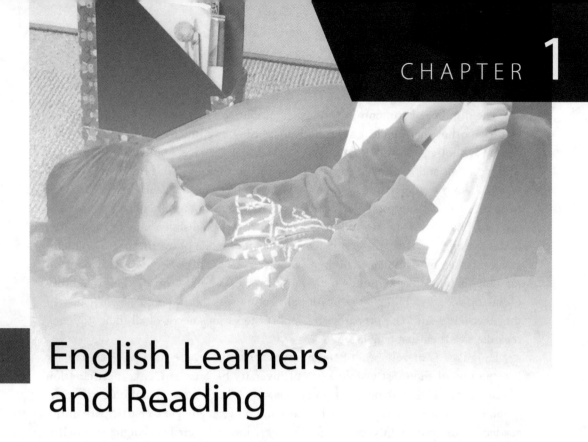

CHAPTER 1

English Learners and Reading

Who Are English Learners?

WAS ENTERING MY THIRD YEAR OF TEACHING AT A SPANISH/ENGLISH BILINGUAL SCHOOL as an English-speaking second-grade teacher, and I was finally starting to feel more confident in my instructional abilities to support my bilingual students. Prior to this year, all of my bilingual students' first language was Spanish, so we were able to provide first-language supports and texts, as well as partners who spoke their first language. As English learners, the students were eager to support each other and often code-switched between English and Spanish. This year, I had a student, Tee, whose first language was Hmong. When our new student did not understand something or did not respond in English, the students would immediately repeat it in Spanish. They were confused initially about the fact that he was learning English, but his first language was not Spanish. This posed an interesting instructional challenge, as I did not have the same resources in Hmong as I did in Spanish. It inspired me to think critically about ways to bring awareness to and acceptance of other languages and cultures and make content comprehensible for all of my bilingual students, even when I did not have bilingual resources.

The number of students entering school who are fortunate enough to speak a language other than English at home is increasing at a much greater rate than the overall school-age population (Office of English Language Acquisition, Language Enhancement and Academic Achievement for Limited English Proficient Students 2010). Like my students, many people hear the term *English learner* (also referred to as *EL* or *ELL*) and immediately think of students who are fluent in Spanish and learning English as their second language. However, English learners in the United States include students whose first language could be one of over four hundred languages spoken by school-age children (Kindler 2002). This presents a wide range of possible linguistic backgrounds for English learners and also limits the probability of having access to bilingual educational experiences for all languages. Because of this, teachers need to be prepared to support the various needs of all their students, regardless of their first language.

Language is merely one of the many ways children are diverse. However, it is often one of the most visible areas of diversity because students' participation in school is so largely dependent on language. Children's social and cultural backgrounds influence who they are as learners and how they begin to participate in the academic community (Vygotsky 1978). Regardless of their first language, English learners come from a wide range of ethnic, cultural, socioeconomic, religious, educational, and literary backgrounds (among many other characteristics). Like monolingual students, no two English learners are the same, and our instruction must change to differentiate and meet the vast needs in diverse elementary classrooms. It is important to note that being an English learner should not be seen as a deficit; rather, it should be seen as students bringing the asset of bilingualism (and hopefully, biliteracy) that our young learners will take with them into college and the workforce.

English learners may be learning English in school, but they already possess linguistic resources that enable them to participate in a range of communicative settings in at least one language (MacSwan, Rolstad, and Glass 2002; Valdés et al. 2005) and have knowledge of conventions and discourses used in their own communities (Gutiérrez, Morales, and Martinez 2009; Gutiérrez and Orellana 2006; Orellana and Gutiérrez 2006). Drawing on their conceptual knowledge in their first language will help support the acquisition of their second language (Cummins 1991). When teachers understand second language acquisition and the broad stages associated with language development and proficiency, they can provide informed instruction to make content comprehensible for all students.

■ Stages of Language Proficiency

A teacher on recess duty said to her teaching partner, with whom she traded students during science, "I am so frustrated with Jorge. Look at him. He is running around, flirting with the girls, and talking incessantly with his friends. Then, when he comes to me for science, he acts like he can barely speak English." The teaching partner explained, "He is really blossoming with his conversational language. Just the last month or so, I have seen him be able to communicate comfortably with his peers and me. He is still working hard on some of the school- and content-specific language. He might just need a little more support with the language and new content because it isn't language he is encountering outside the classroom."

This vignette represents a conversation I initially overheard as a classroom teacher. However, I have heard a different version of this story from many teachers as they struggle with understanding the nuances of second language acquisition and language proficiency levels. Language proficiency is based on a student's ability to read, write, speak, and listen in her second language (for the purposes of this text, English). Language proficiency is related to English learners' conversational and academic communicative skills (Cummins 1991). English learners begin to develop Basic Interpersonal Communicative Skills (BICS) to communicate and understand what is said in typical conversations (Cummins 1991). In addition to BICS, English learners also develop Cognitive Academic Language Proficiency (CALP), which refers to the formal academic language they need to be successful in school settings. Although English learners can develop conversational and academic language simultaneously in the classroom setting, academic proficiency can take anywhere from four to ten years, whereas conversational proficiency may be acquired in only one to three years (Cummins 2008, 2003; Hakuta, Butler, and Witt 2000). Their BICS proficiency can often be misinterpreted as overall proficiency, similar to the teacher's perception of Jorge.

Scholars have identified various levels/stages of language proficiency through which typical English learners progress (Krashen and Terrell 1983). The language proficiency levels listed in Figure 1.1 draw on the initial development of levels as well as adaptations from other experts (e.g., Freeman and Freeman 2000; Kendall and Khuon 2005) and the *Teachers of English to Speakers of Other Languages* (TESOL) standards (2006). Like any proficiency level identification, it is rare that an individual falls completely into one level and displays all of the characteristics thought to correspond with the level. Additionally, these levels do not correspond with age or grade level. You might have a Bridging first grader or a Starting fifth grader. These levels of proficiency described in Figure 1.1 are used as a guideline to begin thinking about what you know about your English learners and how you can best support them. Throughout Chapters Three, Four, Five, Six, and Seven, I provide ideas for differentiation according to the proficiency levels/stages explained in Figure 1.1.

Stages of Language Proficiency	Description
STAGE 1: *Preproduction* Silent Period (Starting)	Students are in a silent period in which they listen, but do not speak in English. They may respond using nonverbal cues in an attempt to communicate basic needs.
STAGE 2: *Early Production* (Emerging)	Students are beginning to understand more oral language. They respond using one- or two-word phrases and start to produce simple sentences for basic social interactions and to meet basic needs.
STAGE 3: *Speech Emergence* (Developing)	Students' listening comprehension improves, and they can understand written English. Students are fairly comfortable engaging in social conversations using simple sentences, but they are just beginning to develop their academic language proficiency.
STAGE 4: *Intermediate Fluency* (Expanding)	Students understand and frequently use conversational English with relatively high accuracy. Their academic vocabulary is expanding, but they still need support with contextualization of abstract concepts. They are able to communicate their ideas in both oral and written contexts.
STAGE 5: *Advanced Fluency* (Bridging)	Students comprehend and engage in conversational and academic English with proficiency. They perform near grade level in reading, writing, and other content areas.

Adapted from Opitz and Guccione (2009)

Figure 1.1 *Stages of Language Proficiency*

It is essential that English learners, regardless of their language proficiency level, are exposed to grade-level content and literacy-rich experiences. However, teachers must find ways to support *all* students in their content knowledge, language, and literacy development. Throughout the book, I provide instructional ideas, lesson examples, and differentiation ideas and I suggest children's literature to give teachers some ideas for getting started in supporting English learners in the reading workshop.

■ Academic Performance of English Learners

Studies reveal that native English speakers tend to score better than English learners on academic assessments in English (National Assessment of Educational Progress 2009). Comprehension challenges in English can be attributed to limited background knowledge and underdeveloped vocabulary in English learners' second language (Bradley and Bryant 1983; Muter et al. 2004; National Research Council 1997). These statistics largely ignore the strengths and assets English learners bring in their first language, but they are also representative of what "counts" on standardized assessments. Through a deeper understanding of language acquisition and specific considerations for content and language development, teachers can use a reading workshop model to build on English learners' strengths and knowledge to better facilitate meaningful language and literacy experiences.

Historically, many English learners receive decontextualized, rote-based instruction focused on skill acquisition (Allington 1991; Darling-Hammond 1995) and are more frequently placed in lower-ability groups than native English speakers (Ruiz-de-Velasco and Fix 2000). This emphasis on language as a form robs English learners of the opportunity to draw on the variety of potential resources they already possess, such as background knowledge related to the reading topic, reading comprehension strategies, interests, and motivation (Bernhardt 2011). "ELLs learn language as they engage in meaningful content-rich activities (projects, presentations, investigations) that encourage language growth through perception, interaction, planning, research, discussion, argument, and co-construction of academic products" (Hakuta and Santos 2012, iii). These meaningful content-rich activities are the foundation for supporting English learners in the reading workshop.

■ English Learners and the Common Core

The Common Core State Standards (National Governors Association Center for Best Practices and Council of the Chief State School Officers 2010b) that focus on critical thinking, research, and complex texts provide both challenges and opportunities for supporting the language and literacy development for elementary-age English learners. The CCSS includes some general guidelines in an ancillary document on the website (www.corestandards.org) for applying the standards to English learners. They recommend that schools provide:

- appropriate instructional supports to make grade-level course work comprehensible
- modified assessments that allow English learners to demonstrate their content knowledge
- additional time for English learners to complete tasks and assessments
- opportunities for classroom interactions (both listening and speaking) that develop concepts and academic language in the disciplines
- opportunities for English learners to interact with proficient English speakers

- opportunities for English learners to build on their strengths, prior experiences, and background knowledge
- qualified teachers who use practices found to be effective in improving student achievement (National Governors Association Center for Best Practices and Council of the Chief State School Officers 2010a).

Although these recommendations may help English learners meet the standards, they provide a vague guideline for teachers. With these types of guidelines, I find myself asking, "Yes, but what does that look like in practice?" Hakuta identifies two essential elements necessary to provide specific support for teachers related to the recommendations in the CCSS: providing English learners with the mainstream academic content that all students receive and assisting English learners in acquiring English proficiency, particularly both oral and written CALP that is foundational to the content standards (as cited in Migdol 2011). In the following chapters, you'll find ideas, lessons, and examples of what this looks like in linguistically diverse reading workshops in elementary classrooms.

■ Effective Instruction for English Learners

"What does effective instruction for English learners look like? How can I best support *all* my students—both English learners and native English speakers? What should I prioritize to begin implementing in my classroom immediately?" These are questions I regularly hear from teachers as they begin to reflect on improving instruction for their English learners. There are many ways these questions will be addressed throughout the book, but I am going to begin with my top five tips for supporting English learners in the reading workshop.

■ Top Five Tips for Supporting English Learners in a Reading Workshop

Each tip is based on a component of successful instruction for English learners as documented by research. I have selected these ideas not only based on research but also based on personal experience and observation as they were implemented in my own classroom or classrooms of teachers with whom I have worked.

Tip #1. Build a Classroom Community: Supportive Spaces

An essential component of successful programs for English learners is the importance of meaningful interactions between teachers and pupils with the use of cooperative learning (e.g., Berman et al. 1995; Doherty et al. 2003; Montecel and Cortez 2002). It is through these meaningful interactions that we establish a classroom community where students feel safe to explore, discuss, and take risks in their first and/or second language. Deep thinking, interpretation, and analysis take place when individuals have the opportunity to interact without the fear of being wrong or ridiculed for their thoughts. If we want students to "go deeper" with their reading, writing, speaking, and listening, we must ensure an environment that supports it both socially and academically.

One way to accomplish this academically is to provide students with choices for texts, topics, and responses. Although many teachers are concerned about text readability and students' reading levels, Halladay (2008, 2012) reports that many students can read above their reading level when the topic is of interest. Likewise, English learners have demonstrated higher motivation and engagement when given choice for topic, texts, and ways to respond to texts (Guccione 2010). In addition to choice, modeling the sharing of "incorrect" or "out-of the box" thinking demonstrates it is safe to share our work and thinking in progress. It is through dialogue and negotiation that we learn more about the language and content. As students begin to feel safe, we are able to lower their "affective filter" (Krashen 1987). The *affective filter* refers to the anxiety or emotions that may affect their ability for input to be understood and retained. When students are in high-stress situations and do not feel comfortable, their affective filter will be high, and they will not be able to understand and retain as much information as they would in a supportive classroom community.

Tip #2. Encourage Discussion: Chatter Matters

English learners excel in a language-rich environment where they have the opportunity to hear and participate in meaningful discussions. To acquire another language, learners need to use it. As they are actively engaged in conversations, they can make connections necessary for learning. This might begin with encouraging conversational English related to feelings or connections to literature they are reading. Whole-class, small-group, and individual conversations can facilitate the development of both conversational and academic English in nonthreatening ways.

Dialogue about matters of interest and concern to English learners should be used to foster their curiosity and desire to learn. English learners benefit from a collaborative community where students not only learn language but also develop knowledge and understanding with and from each other by engaging in dialogue (Wells 1999). Conversations surrounding topics of interest and common texts create positive attitudes toward reading while simultaneously addressing and supporting listening and reading comprehension.

Tip #3. Implement Meaningful, Consistent, Thematically Integrated Curriculum: Insightful Instruction

Teaching skills in isolation creates a confusing and disjointed vision of what it means to be literate. The purpose of teaching skills (decoding, comprehension, etc.) is not for students to be able to demonstrate that skill, but rather to provide students with tools to more effectively engage with texts. Successful programs for English learners implement meaningful and academically challenging curriculum with an emphasis on higher-order thinking (Berman et al. 1995; Doherty et al. 2003; Montecel and Cortez 2002). As we facilitate interactive discussions about meaningful content, we must encourage students to move beyond the literal by modeling and encouraging the independent use of higher-order thinking.

For this curriculum to be effective, it needs to be consistent over time (Ramirez 1992) and thematically integrated (Montecel and Cortez 2002). A reading workshop model lends itself to consistent and thematically integrated instruction through thoughtful units of study supported by whole-group anchor lessons, workshop learning experiences, small-group instruction, and word work, conferring, and reflection. As students begin to understand the connectedness of their literary experiences and develop stronger language and literacy skills, they are able to engage in critical discussions about literature interpretations and analysis.

Tip #4. Focus on Content and Language Instruction: Balancing Both

It is not a focus on content *or* language; it is both! Students learn language through content and content through language. These knowledge bases support each other and develop simultaneously for English learners. English learners possess a great deal of background knowledge and life experiences that can be used to further develop their language proficiency. As content is presented and explored, they can draw on their prior knowledge from their first language to make the content in English comprehensible. As teachers, we can design lessons and learning experiences that enhance students' abilities to better understand the academic content and English language. The key is being purposeful about your objectives for the content and language learning.

Echevarria and colleagues (2008) have identified multiple successful instruction adaptations for supporting English learners. They suggest making explicit the content and language objectives (these are separate) for each lesson. Other suggestions include modifying speech, using contextual clues, providing multisensory experiences, using comprehensible input, conducting frequent comprehension checks, assessing with formative and summative measures, and creating content-driven, developmentally appropriate lessons for English learners. All of these are important aspects to consider when designing units of study and lesson plans in your linguistically diverse reading workshop.

Tip #5. Use Assessment to Guide Instruction and Differentiation: Ideal Individualization

Successful instruction for English learners clearly and consistently aligns with standards and assessment (Doherty et al. 2003; Montecel and Cortez 2002). Teachers can use data from formal and informal assessments to guide their instructional decisions to address standards and meet the needs of their students. Teachers can ask themselves, "What do I want to know? Why do I want to know it? How can I best discover it?" (Opitz and Guccione 2009). Beyond the formal assessments, teachers can gain a deeper understanding of English learners' language and literacy competencies by examining student work, observing student discussions, and conferring with students. A broad explanation of implications for literacy instruction and differentiation according to proficiency level can be found in Figure 1.2.

Stages of Language Proficiency	Implications for Literary Instruction
STAGE 1: *Preproduction Silent Period (Starting)*	Oral reading should be modeled by the teacher and other students. Students in the silent period should not be forced to speak, but should be given the opportunity to try, if they want, in a group activity where they won't be singled out.
STAGE 2: *Early Production (Emerging)*	Teacher and students should continue to model oral reading. Students should be encouraged to begin taking risks with simple, rehearsed reading and discussion in nonthreatening situations.
STAGE 3: *Speech Emergence (Developing)*	Students continue to learn through modeling. Students should participate in whole-class, small-group, partner, and rehearsed reading, writing, and discussion activities. They will need support and opportunities to practice with feedback before independent or paired sharing or reading for an audience.
STAGE 4: *Intermediate Fluency (Expanding)*	With scaffolding, students can successfully participate in most literacy activities that native speakers are expected to complete. Open-ended questions will allow students to demonstrate comprehension and academic language development.
STAGE 5: *Advanced Fluency (Bridging)*	Students should be encouraged to use higher-level thinking skills during their oral reading. They are near native-like proficiency in oral reading, but may still need support with analyzing, inferring, and evaluating.

Adapted from Opitz and Guccione (2009)

Figure 1.2 *Implications for Literacy Instruction*

Reflection

☐ What are some ways you can build on the many cultural and linguistic resources your students bring to school?

☐ Consider how you are currently assessing English learners' stages of language proficiency. What additional informal measures might you use to assess their constantly growing language development?

☐ What are some instructional ideas for moving away from rote-based instruction focused on skills to meaningful content-rich activities?

☐ After reading the top five tips for supporting English learners, identify the following two things in relation to each tip: (1) the ways in which you are already implementing aspects of instructional tips, and (2) the ways in which you could enhance and expand on this idea in your classroom.

CHAPTER 2

Structure of the Reading Workshop for English Learners and Common Questions

I WAS IN THE AIRPORT ON MY WAY HOME FROM THREE DAYS OF CONSULTING IN Baltimore when I ran into a new colleague from my university. She asked what I had been doing, and I told her, "I am doing some long-term professional development work with an elementary school here related to supporting English learners in the reading workshop." She asked me if reading workshop was an intervention program. I paused and realized just how solidified I had become in using my literacy education jargon. It was a valid question, and when many people think about supporting English learners or "struggling" readers, they instantly think of a specific and explicit intervention program. As I tried to give a brief explanation of the reading workshop, I explained it was not a program, but more of a framework to guide authentic and individualized instruction. When she asked what I meant by *authentic* instruction, I explained the instruction should be based on students' language and literacy needs for engaging with texts independently, as opposed to a focus on sequenced skills.

This conversation left me thinking about how important it is for me to be able to articulate what reading workshop is and how it benefits English learners. The challenge is that reading workshop is not a simple instructional strategy that can be summed up in a sentence or two. It is a complex and ever-changing way to think about using best practices to guide children on their literacy journeys. This becomes even more complex when you add additional languages as considerations for instruction, differentiation, and individualization. In this chapter, I share a very basic overview of the reading workshop, its components, and additional components and considerations for supporting English learners in the reading workshop. Then, I address the three most frequently asked questions I hear when working with teachers on supporting English learners in the reading workshop.

Reading Workshop

Many reading workshop experts and scholars agree on a similar framework that includes the broad units of study as a guiding theme or concepts for extended learning. According to these scholars, the following learning opportunities take place on most days: brief teacher-guided lesson (also sometimes called *minilesson*), independent reading/work with choice, small-group work, conferring, and sharing (Calkins 2010; Serafini 2001; Serravallo 2010; Taberski 2000). The reading workshop is largely based on the effective instructional approach of the gradual release of responsibility (Pearson and Gallagher 1983) in that it begins with teacher modeling followed by guided practice and eventually, independent application. I give a brief overview of each of the reading workshop components. Then, building on my top five tips for supporting English learners found in Chapter One, I share how I modify the "standard" components to meet the needs of English learners and share where you can find more detail about this aspect in the following chapters.

Units of Study

The workshop framework has a highly predictable structure beginning with a brief minilesson followed by self-selected independent reading (and related "work" in some cases). During the independent reading, also often referred to as the "workshop time," the teacher meets with small groups and confers with individual students. At the end of the period, there is some type of share and reflection from the day's reading workshop. Units of study provide a framework for connected and cohesive instruction over time that includes this predictable structure on a daily basis. These units could range in focus from genre studies to author studies to character studies. Depending on the age and needs of the students, teachers can adjust accordingly.

When planning units of study for classrooms with English learners, I recommend planning for various language proficiency levels. This includes setting both content and language objectives for the unit. Taking into consideration the goals and objectives related to language for English learners can be crucial when designing lessons, selecting texts, creating guided learning experiences, facilitating independent practice, and meeting with small groups. Building on the unit objectives, I also recommend preplanning general differentiation ideas for students in each stage of language proficiency throughout the unit. This provides an up-front opportunity to plan for support, modifications, small-group instruction, and one-on-one coaching. This is addressed in greater detail with additional considerations for English learners in Chapter Three.

Teacher-Guided Lessons/Minilessons

Teacher-guided lessons or minilessons are exactly what they sound like. This is where the teacher introduces an essential skill or concept that will be helpful to readers in their independent reading. Calkins (2010) and Serravallo (2010) recommend seven- to ten-minute minilessons to introduce these skills or concepts. They suggest presenting a connection, teaching the skill, engaging students in active involvement, and linking it to students' independent reading. This is a strong model for lessons to start the workshop, but I have adjusted it slightly for supporting English learners based on my classroom experiences and work with teachers in multilingual classrooms. I still regularly use minilessons for some whole-group instruction and much of my small-group instruction, but I have found I also need lessons that build community and foster deeper thinking, discussion, exploration, and engagement with literature. I find this often takes more than seven to ten minutes, particularly when adding additional language scaffolds, opportunities for talk, and that crucial "wait time" so English learners can process.

I call these lessons "anchor lessons" because they are the anchor of introducing and mentoring students in the larger context of literacy development. They are introductions to ways of thinking, talking, exploring, and experiencing literature in the social and academic context of our classroom community. Yes, they always include some type of skill or concept that can be used to support their independent reading and/or discussion and reflections to reading, but they also include a read-aloud and time for discussion, reflection, and guided practice with peers. Selecting culturally relevant texts and/or texts with which students have a great deal of background knowledge can help support English learners' understanding of both the text and the lesson. Sample anchor lessons and ideas for planning, differentiation for language proficiency levels, assessment, and children's literature suggestions are discussed in greater detail in Chapter Four.

Independent Reading with Choice

The majority of students' time during the reading workshop should be spent reading books of their choice. To be clear, this does not mean a first grader who is working on learning to decode short vowel sounds should be independently reading *Charlotte's Web*. Students should have a bag or box filled with self-selected books they are able to read independently. I recommend having students visit the classroom library or school library to refill and exchange books for each week. Typically, independent reading time directly follows the minilesson or anchor lesson and students can apply the newly learned skill to their independent reading. Often, some type of reading response is required; this might include sticky notes with strategy use, stop-and-jots, or a reading response journal. Some workshop teachers require that all students are working independently during this time, but I have found it beneficial to give additional options for classrooms with English learners.

For supporting English learners' vast needs in the reading workshop, I suggest what I call "guided learning experiences" during the workshop time. Students still choose their own texts, but they also have a choice in how they spend their time and how they respond to text. As I introduce reading strategies, models for reading (whisper reading, partner reading, big book pointer reading, silent reading, reading along at a listening center, etc.), and ways to respond to text during anchor lessons, I add these to a menu of options for students to use during their independent workshop time. These are all purposeful, guided learning opportunities created to facilitate literacy and language development for English learners during their workshop time. Additional descriptions and menus for guided learning experiences for English learners are described in depth in Chapter Five.

Small-Group Instruction

Small-group instruction is an essential part of most literacy approaches and programs. There are many different options for how to use your time during small-group instruction. Oftentimes, students are pulled together in needs-based groups. This is an important time to target needed instruction, but students, particularly English learners, also need opportunities to participate in heterogeneous and/or interest-based group settings. Small-group instruction should support English learners in many ways including guided reading, strategy instruction, vocabulary instruction, sheltering/

front-loading/reviewing, supported literature circles, fluency, and word work or decoding skills. This targeted instruction in small-group settings can provide the support necessary to successfully participate in whole-group reading and discussion in addition to fostering independence during the guided learning experiences workshop time. Chapter Six provides additional details and examples for small-group instruction that supports English learners.

Sharing

Providing time at the end of the workshop for sharing, reflection, or celebration is a common aspect of various reading workshop models (Calkins 2010; Serravallo 2010; Serafini 2006). This is a time for students to reflect on their learning and workshop experiences. Sharing includes opportunities for teachers and students to discuss reflections, successes, and challenges related to the work during workshop time. In my experiences, this is the most common component that is overlooked and/or underused. It is not purposefully ignored, but teachers report (I am also guilty of this) running out of time and because it is the final aspect, it sometimes gets left out as the students have to be rushed off to recess, lunch, or specials.

Like the other components of reading workshop, I completely support the core idea of reflection and sharing time. However, I also think there are additional considerations, support, and differentiation that can be utilized to assist English learners in successful participation. I separate reflection and sharing into the two categories of daily and culminating event. This allows teachers and English learners to check in with daily successes, challenges, questions, and progress while also considering the final culminating project that is a representation of their long-term learning throughout the course of the unit of study. The reflection and sharing should be related to reading as a content *and* language development. Setting objectives, revisiting objectives, reflecting, and discussing challenges and successes should be focused on both reading and second language acquisition. This focus and discussion helps English learners develop metacognition about their daily progress and progress toward a culminating project that demonstrates their learning and growth in reading and English. Greater discussion and examples from multiple classrooms are shared in Chapter Seven.

Three Most Frequently Asked Questions

I have been fortunate to work with many schools across the United States that are supporting students from a wide range of socioeconomic, racial, and linguistic backgrounds. As teachers embark on their journeys of improving instruction to meet the needs of their ever-changing classrooms, I have been lucky to work alongside them and provide professional development for supporting English learners (and all learners) in the reading workshop. During the last few years of this work together, there are three questions that almost always come up during our first day together. The questions are practical and reflect the teachers' commitment to supporting students within their specific school or district context. They are related to differentiation, logistics of scheduling/organization, and accountability to standards. In the following sections, I share my responses to these questions.

What exactly do you mean by differentiation? How can I differentiate for my English learners?

Differentiation seems to be quite the educational buzzword, and it should be. Essentially, all teachers should be differentiating for their students. No two students or two classes are the same. Although there are similarities, students come in with a wide range of skills and background knowledge from which to build on for effective, targeted instruction right in their Zone of Proximal Development (Vygotsky 1978). Although this makes sense and most teachers already know this, the question is really about logistics: What does differentiation look like? How do I do it? How do I differentiate for my English learners?

I typically introduce four versions of thinking about differentiation when working with teachers. I discuss the four models described by Opitz and Ford (2008) in *Doable Differentiation*. Then, I go on to talk about the more complex and complicated differentiation techniques presented by Tomlinson's (2001) extensive work with differentiation. I ask teachers to consider Serafini's (2012) differentiation considerations model. I share with them my suggestions for differentiation according to language proficiency stages. Finally, I quote Tim Gunn and tell them to "Make it work!" Differentiation should be about adjusting instruction to optimally meet the needs of diverse learners. No one model will work perfectly in every classroom, so basically, I encourage teachers to differentiate the differentiation models for themselves.

There are entire books on differentiation, so I will only give a brief overview here. Opitz and Ford (2008) present four models for differentiation: grouping without tracking; jigsaw; connected literature circles; and focused readers' workshop. Each model considers ways to differentiate according to text, grouping, and support. Tomlinson (2001) presents a more complex process as she recommends differentiation through content, process, product, and affect/environment according to students' readiness, interest, and learning profile. She advocates creating a high-interest activity, charting it along a complexity ladder, and then cloning the activity along the ladder to meet the needs of individual learners. Serafini (2012) argues that differentiation is really a matter of differentiating (or modifying) texts, teaching, tasks, time, talk, and/or context.

Building on all of these models, I share my differentiation chart that was created specifically for teachers of English learners. It is organized according to language proficiency levels. This chart is based on the approximate levels and literacy instructional implications reported in Figures 1.1 and 1.2. I encourage teachers to think about the teacher roles (how they can modify instruction to support English learners) and students' expectations (what they can realistically expect their English learners to do and work toward). After sharing examples I have used in my classroom and when working with teachers (as seen in Chapters Four, Five, Six, and Seven), I encourage teachers to start with an anchor lesson they have planned and then use this model to plan their roles and English learner expectations based on what they now know about their options for differentiation from all of the introduced models. Teachers should use their professional knowledge to create a scale or spectrum of differentiation for their students. I try to encourage teachers to put language acquisition at the forefront of their differentiation considerations.

What are some possible schedules? How do I fit it all in?

Let me start by saying there is no one right way to schedule your reading workshop. Many different daily and weekly structures can be effective for supporting English learners in the reading workshop. I am going to present a few schedules I have seen work in various classrooms, but similar to differentiation, teachers have to find a way to make it work in their own setting. The outline of the schedules will be a general and conservative one. Many schools designate two hours for literacy instruction, especially in the primary grades. However, to err on the side of caution, the general daily schedule is going to be based on a ninety-minute reading block. I find most classrooms have at least ninety minutes devoted to reading. Based on that assumption, here's a schedule that includes an introduction, an anchor lesson, guided learning experiences workshop time with small-groups and conferring, and a reflection and sharing time.

- Introduction: The introduction includes connections to previous learning and content and language objective presentation (3–5 minutes).
- Anchor lesson: The anchor lesson involves modeling and guided practice (15–20 minutes, though some days may be longer while others just include a brief minilesson).

- Guided learning experiences workshop time: Students work from their guided learning experiences menu to read and apply skills (independently or in partners or small groups) while the teacher confers and meets with small groups (60 minutes).
- Reflection and sharing: Students and teachers review objectives, reflect, share successes and challenges, and participate in discussion of the workshop (5–10 minutes).

For most teachers this schedule seems manageable. Their biggest concern is how and when to fit in the conferring and different types of small-group instruction. Many teachers are accustomed to an hour block to meet with small groups during which they meet with leveled groups and conduct guided reading, strategy instruction, or a combination of both. The idea of adding conferring and changing groups to make them flexible can cause scheduling anxiety. I share two possible schedules in Figures 2.1 and 2.2. The first is more predictably structured than the second, but both allow time for needs-based word work, guided reading, strategy instruction, interest-based literature circles (or book club), and conferring.

The first weekly small-group and conferring schedule seen in Figure 2.1 is based on four needs-based groups that were created according to observations and assessments. The teacher revisits the groups as necessary and formally every six weeks after a new testing period. All students receive word work, guided reading, and strategy instruction Monday through Thursday. The teacher uses word work, strategy instruction, and conferring time to provide additional language and vocabulary support for English learners. All students are also involved in an interest-based book club/literature circle that meets once a week on Monday, Wednesday, or Friday. They conduct their reading and response preparation during independent workshop and at home. When they are not in small groups, they are working from the menu of options for guided learning experiences. This leaves the teacher approximately seventy-five minutes for one-on-one conferences throughout the week.

The second example found in Figure 2.2 also includes a schedule that has seventy-five minutes for conferring and meeting with needs-based groups for word work, guided reading, and strategy instruction. However, this schedule differs in a couple of ways. First, the teacher only does a five-minute check-in with the interest-based literature circles. Additionally, she writes in who will be in each group at the beginning of the week, and groups change regularly based on what she observes. The groups are not the same for word work, guided reading, and strategy instruction. She changes those based on the daily and weekly needs demonstrated by her students. She also includes a beginning of the week and midweek English language support group to reinforce and scaffold concepts from the anchor lesson, provide targeted language support as necessary, and foster greater independence for her English learners.

	Monday	Tuesday	Wednesday	Thursday	Friday
Word Work (15 minutes)	Group 1	Group 2	Group 3	Group 4	
Guided Reading (15 minutes)	Group 4	Group 1	Group 2	Group 3	
Strategy Instruction (15 minutes)	Group 3	Group 4	Group 1	Group 2	
Interest-Based Literature Circles (15 minutes)	Junie B.		Frog and Toad		Flat Stanley
Conferring (15–45 minutes)		15 minutes		15 minutes	45 minutes

Figure 2.1 *Example 1 Schedule*

	Monday	Tuesday	Wednesday	Thursday	Friday
Word Work	15 minutes	15 minutes		15 minutes	15 minutes
Guided Reading	15 minutes	15 minutes	15 minutes		15 minutes
Strategy Instruction		15 minutes	15 minutes	15 minutes	15 minutes
Interest-Based Literature Circles	Book 1 (check-in 5 minutes)		Book 2 (check-in 5 minutes)		Book 3 (check-in 5 minutes)
ELL Support	15 minutes		15 minutes		
Conferring	10 minutes	15 minutes	10 minutes	30 minutes	10 minutes

Figure 2.2 *Example 2 Schedule*

These are merely two examples of how teachers structured small groups and workshop time with special considerations for supporting English learners in the workshop model. I have also seen teachers use guided reading or word work on an as-needed basis as they see fit for their students. Their small-group time was based on a daily observation of immediate needs and support. The key is making it work within the requirements of your school and district in a way that supports your English learners. Targeted small-group instruction and conferring will maximize student progress, but it takes up-front planning and scheduling to ensure the needs of all learners are met.

What about the standards?

The simple answer is, "Yes, quality instruction and the reading workshop address the standards." The more nuanced answer includes taking a look at how this instruction addresses the specific standards the teachers are required to use, identifying standards that might not be fully addressed, and designing instruction that includes opportunities to address all of the standards. Most school districts follow some type of "standards-driven" curriculum whether it is a commercial program or the reading and writing workshop. With the rollout of the Common Core State Standards (CCSS), schools seem to have a heightened awareness of the standards. Although some districts have jumped on board with the CCSS, some have rejected the CCSS, and they are using state standards or the National Council of Teachers of English/International Reading Association (NCTE/IRA) English Language Arts Standards. Either way, teachers are being held accountable to address the standards.

As you will see in my unit-planning guide in the following chapter, I include a planning space for standards that will be addressed. In my sample unit planning, I was working with teachers who were required to document how they addressed the CCSS, but this could be adapted to work with any standards (state, *Teachers of English to Speakers of Other Languages*, NCTE/IRA, etc.). Addressing standards can and should be done during daily planning as well, but teachers should have an idea of the standards that will (and will not) be addressed throughout the course of a unit. This will also help over the course of the year as teachers are identifying which standards might need more attention.

I have to admit, I never select standards and then create lessons. I just do not think this is best practice. In fact, I think this can actually be counterintuitive depending on your students. For example, it is not appropriate to be spending the majority of my instructional time teaching how to decode words with common prefixes and suffixes (CCSS, Foundational Skills 3d for second grade) when working with an

English learner just beginning to learn the letter sounds. Students should be exposed to grade-level content, but most instruction, particularly small group and coaching, should be at an instructional level where English learners can participate and have maximized opportunities for growth. This is true for text selection also. As Allington (2000) has documented, students need a great deal of time for reading accessible text to grow as readers. This is true for English learners as well!

I always have the standards in the back of my mind, but I think we have to put the kids in the front of our mind. We should not do away with the standards, but we need to look at the students in front of us, assess their strengths and needs, and provide appropriate instruction. I have found this type of student-centered instruction typically addresses all the standards. I encourage documenting the standards as they are addressed and using them as a gauge for where you started, how far you have come, and where you are headed.

Reflection

- ☐ What components of the reading workshop are included in your classroom instruction?
- ☐ How can you adapt your reading workshop to better support the needs of your English learners?
- ☐ Consider differentiation roles of the teacher and English learner expectations. How might you plan for and implement differentiated instruction to support the needs of your English learners?
- ☐ Create a schedule for supporting all students with special considerations for English learners in the reading workshop given your specific classroom context and schedule constraints. Include time for anchor lessons, various small groups, conferring, independent work, and reflection and sharing. How will you allocate your time? How will you provide additional language considerations and supports?
- ☐ How will you plan for and address the standards?

CHAPTER 3

Units of Study

" I T JUST SEEMS SO UNORGANIZED—EVERYONE READING DIFFERENT BOOKS, different options for their work, different groupings. How can you have cohesion and consistency when students are always choosing their own books? Half of my kids are just learning English. I think, why not go with the basals? Everything we need is already planned, sequenced, and ready for us." As I was working with a group of teachers discussing curriculum development and a shift from a commercially produced curriculum to the reading and writing workshop, a veteran teacher voiced these concerns. Many teachers have similar questions when moving to a student-centered curricular approach, especially when working with English learners. I had a few misconceptions to clarify before we could get started on our work together.

The first misconception was that the reading workshop is unorganized. Actually, a well-run workshop is the opposite. Because students will be receiving differentiated instruction appropriate for their language and literacy abilities and reading and responding with self-selected text, teachers must thoughtfully plan and organize their classroom to support *all* learners. I have never been in a classroom where one lesson with one assignment was "just right" for every student in the classroom. This is even more important for classrooms with English learners. Many strategies and skills transfer across texts, and moving away from the one-size-fits-all model allows for English learners to apply and practice these skills in appropriate and culturally relevant texts that are self-selected by the students (with the teacher's initial guidance, of course).

In this chapter, I provide suggestions for planning and implementing meaningful units of study to support English learners. The units of study are designed for entire classrooms with monolingual speakers and English learners, but the planning, differentiation, small-group, and independent options are meant to support English learners at various levels of proficiency. I first address the planning and facilitation of units of study by explaining the components and providing a broad/general unit planning guide. I share specific examples of planned units of study with informational and poetry texts that include ideas for differentiation according to language proficiency levels. Then, I discuss the importance of conferring with English learners to guide future instruction and differentiation. Finally, I conclude the chapter with practical ideas for assessing students throughout the units of study.

Broad Overview: What is it? Why do we do it? How do we plan for it?

Units of study are constantly recommended as a guiding framework for instruction by many reading and writing workshop experts (Calkins 2001; Ray 2006, Serafini and Serafini-Youngs 2006). But what exactly is a unit of study? Well, depending on whom you ask, the answer will vary. Some say it is a theme around which to base your unit. Others say units of study should be genre-based. I like to think of units of study as the "big ideas" and guiding framework for a cohesive unit. In my classroom, this included author units, thematic units (habitats, making friends, etc.), becoming a reader and building stamina units, units of study on characters, units of inquiry, and genre studies (among many others). Basically, the unit of study should create a focus for common language, predictable structures and routines, common texts from which to teach minilessons, and opportunities for whole-group, small-group, partner, and independent work. It creates cohesion among your daily instruction from which to make connections to students' independent reading and "work." Units can be as brief or long as needed depending on the focus and your students' needs and interests.

Units of study include various components that can be altered based on the needs of your classroom. Figure 3.1 is a unit-planning guide I use when working with teachers and districts generating their own reading workshop curriculum. This planning guide is specific to schools and districts working with English learners, so it incorporates language and content objectives to focus language instruction and goals. Additionally, it includes specific differentiation planning and techniques for students with various language proficiency levels. In the following chapters you will see the Differentiation and Considerations According to Proficiency Levels charts for each of

Central Focus/Unity of Study:

Cornerstone Text:

Standards:

Unit Content Objectives:

Unit Language Objectives:

Anchor Lessons (*involve a read-aloud, cornerstone text, revisiting central focus—BIG IDEAS*):

Guided Learning Experiences/Workshop Time (*will have to be taught originally during whole-group or small-group time*):

Workshop Menu Options:

Small-Group Instruction/Word Work:

Reflection and Sharing (*daily and culminating experience*):

Assessment/Documentation:

Text Sets (*books needed for whole-group, small-group, and independent reading*):

Differentiation for Proficiency Levels:

Stages of Language Proficiency	Teacher Roles	English Learner Expectations/Performance
STAGE 1: Preproduction Silent Period (Starting)		
STAGE 2: Early Production (Emerging)		
STAGE 3: Speech Emergence (Developing)		
STAGE 4: Intermediate Fluency (Expanding)		
STAGE 5: Advanced Fluency (Bridging)		

Full-size reproducible available at www.heinemann.com/products/E05757.aspx.

Figure 3.1 *Unit Planning*

the suggested lessons. Figure 3.1 is a suggested template for broad unit planning, but it can also be adapted and used for more specific daily planning.

The specifics of each of these components are discussed in detail in the subsequent chapters. However, to create consistent and cohesive units of study for English learners, I suggest incorporating all of these components in the planning and instruction. The focus and consistency of theme or concept in units of study are particularly important and beneficial for English learners. There are many reasons to organize curriculum around themes when teaching in classrooms with English learners. Freeman and Freeman (2000) note the following reasons:

- Students see the big picture so they can make sense of English language instruction.
- Through themes based on big questions, teachers can connect curriculum to students' lives, making curriculum more interesting.
- Because the curriculum makes sense, English-language learners are more fully engaged and experience more success.
- Since themes deal with universal human topics, all students can be involved, and lessons and activities can be adjusted to different levels of English language proficiency. (11)

Thoughtful planning and implementation of units of study are organized and flexible to motivate all learners. I have found this initial stage of planning is crucial to successfully supporting English learners in the reading workshop.

 ## Specific Ideas for Instruction (Poetry and Informational Focus)

In the following sections, I include sample units of study planning guides for primary and intermediate classrooms with informational and poetry texts. These planning guides include all of the components found in Figure 3.1. Following the planning guide information, I include a list of suggested children's literature texts that might complement a similar unit at both primary and intermediate levels. Typically, I meet with grade-level teams and we just type directly into a Word template as seen in Figure 3.1; this seems to make it easier to adjust as necessary throughout the unit. The following units of study are just samples—you can and should adjust standards, goals, lessons, small groups, and culminating experiences to meet the needs of your students and unit focus. For example, the classrooms using these units of study were required to connect to the Common Core State Standards (CCSS), but many districts have chosen to use state standards or the Standards of English Language Arts put out by the National Council of Teachers of English and the International Reading Association. You can adjust this planning guide to fit the specific needs of your classroom.

Another important thing to note is that this is a broad plan to help guide long-term instruction. Once this plan is completed, it is not written in stone. On a daily basis, you should be conferring with and assessing your students' needs to adjust your whole-group, small-group, and individual instruction. This information should guide your daily instruction, whereas the unit of study planning guide is a broad framework to help facilitate meaningful and connected daily instructional planning.

Primary Unit of Study Planning Guide (Informational Texts and Inquiry)

Central Focus/Unity of Study
Informational texts and animal or habitat inquiry

Cornerstone Text
A Rainforest Habitat (Aloian and Kalman 2010)

Standards Addressed

Standards	Grade-Level Specifics (Second Grade)
Key Ideas and Details (2)	Identify the main topic of a multiparagraph text as well as the focus of specific paragraphs within the text.
Key Ideas and Details (3)	Describe the connection between a series of historical events, scientific ideas or concepts, or steps in technical procedures in a text.
Craft and Structure (4)	Determine the meaning of words and phrases in a text relevant to a grade 2 topic or subject area.
Craft and Structure (5)	Know and use various text features (e.g., captions, bold print, subheadings, glossaries, indexes, electronic menus, icons) to locate key facts or information in a text efficiently.
Craft and Structure (6)	Identify the main purpose of a text, including what the author wants to answer, explain, or describe.
Integration of Knowledge and Ideas (7)	Explain how specific images contribute to and clarify a text.
Range of Reading and Level of Text Complexity (10)	By the end of year, read and comprehend informational texts, including history/social studies, science, and technical texts, in the grades 2–3 text complexity band proficiently, with scaffolding as needed at the high end of the range.

Unit Content Objectives

☐ I can understand informational text structure and features.

☐ I can utilize research skills to collect information and answer curiosities.

☐ I can share research with peers.

Unit Language Objectives

☐ I can read informational texts.

☐ I can write questions and new information for research posters.

☐ I can orally present research poster to peers.

Anchor Lessons

Nonfiction text features (image/illustration, label, caption, headings, table of contents, index, glossary, diagram, summary, bold print)

Asking questions

Finding answers

Summarizing

Editing

Organizing posters

Presentation practice

Guided Learning Experiences/Workshop Time

Working through the inquiry process by reading, writing, and utilizing strategies of documentation learned in anchor lessons

WORKSHOP MENU OPTIONS:

Sample Checklist for an Inquiry Project Menu		
☐ Questions	☐ I learned	☐ Presentation plan
☐ I think	☐ Connections	☐ Written feedback
☐ Illustrations	☐ Captions	☐ Author info
☐ Labels	☐ Diagrams	☐ Maps
☐ Models	☐ Cutaways	☐ Editing checklist
☐ Summaries	☐ Report	☐ Key terms
☐ Sources	☐ Glossary	☐ Headings
☐ Bibliography	☐ Charts	☐ Annotated bibliography

Small-Group Instruction/Word Work

GROUP 1: Text selection, supported reading, vocabulary support, nonfiction text feature support (table of contents, index, images, labels, captions), documenting new learning (questions, I learned, illustrations, labels, captions), editing, presentation support

GROUP 2: Text selection, supported reading, vocabulary support, nonfiction text feature support (table of contents, index, images, labels, captions, headings, bold print, summaries, sources, diagrams), documenting new learning (questions, I think, I learned, connections, illustrations, labels, captions, sources), editing, presentation support

GROUP 3: Text selection, supported reading, vocabulary support, nonfiction text feature support (table of contents, index, images, labels, captions, headings, bold print, summaries, glossary, sources, diagrams), documenting new learning [questions, I think, I learned, connections (text, world, and self), illustrations, labels, captions, summaries, glossary, sources], editing, presentation support

Reflection and Sharing (Daily and Culminating Experience)

DAILY: Inquiry notebook goal setting and partner check in—sharing progress, new learning, and emerging research posters

CULMINATING: Small-group peer sharing with written and oral feedback; research night presentations for parents and community

Assessment/Documentation

Formative observations, conferring, inquiry menu checklist/rubric, final project, and presentation evaluation

Differentiation and Considerations According to Proficiency Levels

Stages of Language Proficiency	Teacher Roles	English Learner Expectations/Performance
STAGE 1: *Preproduction* *Silent Period (Starting)*	☐ Read aloud or have a peer read aloud to students. ☐ When possible, pair the student with a classmate who speaks the student's first language. ☐ Focus only on image with the possibility of a copied one- to two-word label. ☐ Rehearse the oral presentation/labeling of picture with student.	☐ Can listen to teacher or partner read aloud. ☐ Can copy or create images. ☐ Can use first language to label or name images. ☐ May be able to copy images and brief labels. ☐ Can create a poster of simple images with labels. ☐ Can point to images and repeat labels after rehearsal.

(continues)

Stages of Language Proficiency *(continued)*	Teacher Roles	English Learner Expectations/Performance
STAGE 2: *Early Production* (Emerging)	☐ Read aloud or have a peer read aloud to students. ☐ Encourage students to document understanding in first and second language when possible with labels and/or captions. ☐ Provide sentence starters for captions. Example: This is a picture of _____. ☐ Focus on image and simple copied labels. Scribe captions when possible and encourage rehearsal and sharing with peers.	☐ Can point to images, labels, and captions. ☐ Can copy or create images with simple labels. ☐ Can attempt to fill in the blank and/or copy the sentence starter. ☐ Can create and share a poster with multiple images with simple labels or brief copied or scribed captions in partners or small groups after having a chance to practice/rehearse.
STAGE 3: *Speech Emergence* (Developing)	☐ Have students participate in a paired reading and discussion about nonfiction text features prior to creating their image, label, and caption. ☐ Encourage students to create 3–5 images and labels (in English). ☐ Ask students to write a caption using the sentence starter provided for 3–5 images (summarizing their new learning). ☐ Ask students to create headings for each of their images with captions. ☐ Encourage rehearsal of image, label, and caption sharing.	☐ Can participate in a partner reading of nonfiction text (appropriate level). ☐ Can identify and replicate image, label, and caption (using sentence starter). ☐ Can create and share poster with headings, 3–5 images, labels, and captions with small or whole group after having a chance to practice/rehearse.
STAGE 4: *Intermediate Fluency* (Expanding)	☐ Have students participate in paired or independent reading. ☐ Encourage use of 4–6 nonfiction text features in their poster creation. ☐ Ask students to create images with 2–5 labels. The caption from their learning should be in their own words, not copied from the text (summarize their learning). ☐ Encourage students to discuss and share with partners, small groups, and whole class.	☐ Can participate in independent or paired reading of grade-level nonfiction texts. ☐ Can identify and use 4–6 nonfiction text features in their poster creation. ☐ Can document new learning by creating images with 2–5 labels and a self-created caption. ☐ Can share writing and thinking with classmates.
STAGE 5: *Advanced Fluency* (Bridging)	☐ Encourage summaries, connections, and 5–8 nonfiction text features to document learning across 3–5 texts.	☐ Can summarize, connect, and document learning using 5–8 nonfiction text features across 3–5 informational texts with cited sources. Can make connections to other animals and habitats. Can write and share an oral presentation to accompany the research poster.

Children's Literature Suggestions (Primary)

Aloain, Molly, and Bobbie Kalman. 2007. *A Rainforest Habitat*. New York: Crabtree Publishing.

Lock, David. 2007. *Animals at Home*. New York: DK Publishing.

Marsh, Laura. 2011. *National Geographic Readers: Ponies*. Washington, D.C.: National Geographic Children's Books.

———. 2012. *National Geographic Readers: Tigers*. Washington, D.C.: National Geographic Children's Books.

Stewart, Melissa. 2009. *National Geographic Readers: Snakes*. Washington, D.C.: National Geographic Children's Books.

Children's Literature Suggestions (Intermediate)

Burnie, David. 2008. *Bird*. New York: DK Publishing.

Carney, Elizabeth. 2011. *Everything Big Cats*. Washington, D.C.: National Geographic Children's Books.

———. 2012. *Everything Dolphins*. Washington, D.C.: National Geographic Children's Books.

Parker, Steve. 2004. *DK Eyewitness Books: Mammal*. New York: DK Publishing.

Spelman, Lucy. 2012. *National Geographic Animal Encyclopedia: 2,500 Animals with Photos, Maps and More!* Washington, D.C.: National Geographic Children's Books.

The students' work in Figures 3.2 and 3.3 was done during similar informational text/ inquiry units of study in diverse classroom settings with English learners. Following our professional development work together, these teachers implemented and documented units of inquiry with their kindergarten and fourth-grade students in Florida and Texas. Figure 3.2 is from Beth Roger's kindergarten classroom where students were using comprehension and inquiry strategies to document their thinking (Buhrow and Upczak Garcia 2006). Finally, Figure 3.3 shows a cheetah research poster from Amy Fletcher's fourth-grade classroom.

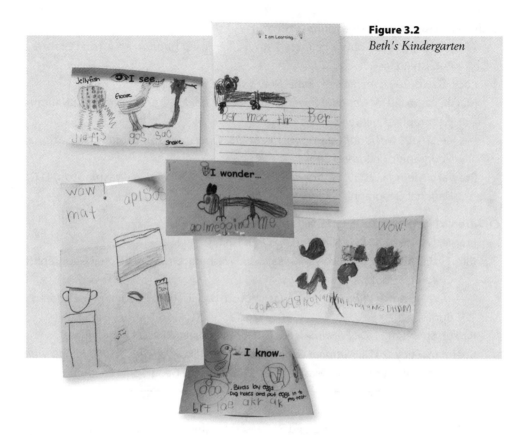

Figure 3.2
Beth's Kindergarten

Intermediate Unit of Study Planning Guide (Poetry)

Central Focus/Unity of Study

Poetry genre study

Cornerstone Text

Sing a Song of Popcorn by Beatrice Schenck de Regniers and Eva Moore

Standards Addressed

Standards	Grade-Level Specifics (Fourth Grade)
Key Ideas and Details (2)	Determine a theme of a story, drama, or poem from details in the text; summarize the text.
Craft and Structure (4)	Determine the meaning of words and phrases as they are used in a text, including those that allude to significant characters found in mythology.

Figure 3.3
Cheetah Poster

Standards *(continued)*	**Grade-Level Specifics (Fourth Grade)**
Craft and Structure (5)	Explain major difference between poems, drama, and prose, and refer to the structural elements of poems and drama when writing or speaking about text.
Integration of Knowledge and Ideas (7)	Make connections between the text of a story or drama and visual or oral presentation of the text, identifying where each version reflects specific descriptions and directions in the text.
Range of Reading and Level of Text Complexity (10)	By the end of year, read and comprehend literature, including stories, dramas, and poetry, in the grades 4–5 text complexity band proficiently, with scaffolding as needed at the high end of the range.

Unit Content Objectives

- ☐ I can identify characteristics of poetry.
- ☐ I can identify at least three different types of poetry.
- ☐ I can compose three different types of poetry.

Unit Language Objectives

- ☐ I can read poetry.
- ☐ I can write poetry.
- ☐ I can orally perform a poem of my choice to peers.

Anchor Lessons

Book/poetry immersion

Poetry characteristics (What do you notice? What purpose does it serve?)

Forms and styles of poetry (acrostic, alphabet, found, haiku, limerick, concrete, sonnet, rhyming, free verse, shape)

Poetry analysis

Poetry book talks

Poetry performance (watching various poetry performances and analyzing prior to students' performances)

Poetry creation

Guided Learning Experiences/Workshop Time

Reading, writing, analyzing, and performing poetry as demonstrated in anchor lessons

OPTIONS:

Poetry scavenger hunt

Independent or partner reading

Poetry notebook

Poetry rehearsal

Poetry performance

Poetry composition

Small-Group Instruction/Word Work

Small groups for this unit will be interest-based and self-selected according to poetry book selection. All groups will receive varying support for the following: supported reading, vocabulary support, fluency support, poetry analysis, poetry book talks, figurative language, poetry composition, editing/feedback, presentation support, and coffeehouse. Conferring, one-on-one support, and needs-based groups will be utilized throughout the unit for individualized instruction.

Reflection and Sharing (Daily and Culminating Experience)

DAILY: Poetry notebook entries and voluntary sharing of poetry, composition or performance

CULMINATING: Coffeehouse performances in small groups (set up classroom like open mic night for poetry performances in three different areas of the room for small groups); students perform a poem of their choice in the small group

Assessment/Documentation

Formative observations, conferring, poetry notebooks, final poetry compositions, and performance evaluation

Differentiation and Considerations According to Proficiency Levels

Stages of Language Proficiency	Teacher Roles	English Learner Expectations/Performance
STAGE 1: *Preproduction Silent Period (Starting)*	☐ Read aloud or have a peer read aloud to students. ☐ When possible, pair the student with a classmate who speaks the student's first language.	☐ Can listen to teacher or partner read aloud. ☐ Can use first language to create poems. ☐ Can perform in first language.
STAGE 2: *Early Production (Emerging)*	☐ Read aloud or have a peer read aloud to students. ☐ When possible, pair the student with a classmate who speaks the student's first language. ☐ Start with simple poems without figurative language. ☐ Provide individual support for poem selection and rehearsal. ☐ Provide audio recordings of poems for rehearsal.	☐ Can listen to teacher or partner read aloud. ☐ Can use first language to create poems. ☐ Can perform in first language. ☐ Can rehearse a haiku or other brief poem in English. Can perform with partner or small group.
STAGE 3: *Speech Emergence (Developing)*	☐ Have students participate in a paired reading and rehearsal of self-selected poems. ☐ Model poem forms and analyzing poems for meaning and style. ☐ Encourage students to write poems in 3 different forms/styles. ☐ Provide feedback on composition and fluency (emphasis on prosody).	☐ Can participate in a partner reading and performances for small group. ☐ Can discuss meaning of poems and identify 2–3 poetry forms. ☐ Can compose poetry in 3 different styles. ☐ Can perform own poetry with adequate fluency.

(continues)

Stages of Language Proficiency *(continued)*	Teacher Roles	English Learner Expectations/Performance
STAGE 4: *Intermediate Fluency (Expanding)*	☐ Have students participate in a paired reading and rehearsal of self-selected poems. ☐ Model poem forms and analyzing poems for meaning and style. Introduce figurative language. ☐ Encourage students to write poems in 4–5 different forms/styles and incorporate figurative language when possible. ☐ Provide feedback on composition and overall performance (fluency and style) for various poems and styles.	☐ Can participate in a partner reading and performances for small group. ☐ Can discuss meaning of poems, identify style and form, and comprehend figurative language. ☐ Can compose poetry in 4–5 different styles. ☐ Can perform own poetry with fluency.
STAGE 5: *Advanced Fluency (Bridging)*	☐ Encourage deeper analysis and comparisons of styles and authors. ☐ Encourage students to write poems with figurative language in 5–7 different styles. ☐ Provide feedback on composition and overall performance.	☐ Can participate in a partner reading and performances for small group. ☐ Can discuss meaning of poems, identify style and form, and comprehend figurative language. ☐ Can compose poetry with figurative language in 5–7 different styles. ☐ Performs with fluency and alters performance and prosody across different styles of poetry.

Children's Literature Suggestions (Primary)

Foxworthy, Jeff. 2009. *Dirt on My Shirt: Selected Poems*. New York: Harper Collins Publishers.

Prelutsky, Jack. 1984. *The New Kid on the Block*. New York: Greenwillow.

Prelutsky, Jack, and Arnold Lobel. 1983. *The Random House Book of Poetry for Children*. New York: Random House.

Silverstein, Shel. 1981. *A Light in the Attic*. New York: Harper Collins Publishers.

White, Mary M., Eva Moore, Beatrice Schenk De Regniers, and Jan Carr. 1988. *Sing a Song of Popcorn*. New York: Scholastic.

Children's Literature Suggestions (Intermediate)

Creech, Sharon. 2010. *Hate That Cat*. New York: Harper Collins.

Hopkins, Lee Bennett, and Chris Soentpiet. 2010. *Amazing Faces*. New York: Lee and Low Books.

Prelutsky, Jack, and Brandon Dorman. 2008. *Be Glad Your Nose Is on Your Face: And Other Poems: Some of the Best of Jack Prelutsky.* New York: Greenwillow Books.

White, Mary M., Eva Moore, Beatrice Schenk De Regniers, and Jan Carr. 1988. *Sing a Song of Popcorn.* New York: Scholastic.

Wilson, Edwin Graves, and Jerome Lagarrigue. 2013. *Poetry for Young People: Maya Angelou.* New York: Sterling Children's Books.

Often poetry is omitted in the younger grades and with English learners, so I wanted to share an example of how this unit of study could be altered to work in a first-grade classroom with English speakers and English learners. In Figure 3.4, two students (one English speaker and one English learner) are rehearsing for their performance. You can also see a list of poetry styles they have learned (cinquain, acrostic, alphabetic, concrete) and the poetry language objectives posted in the background: "We can read and write different kinds of poems."

Figure 3.4
Rehearsal

■ Conferring

Conferring, also called *conferencing* by some, is an essential part of the reading work-shop (Calkins 2001; Serafini and Serafini-Youngs 2006) with entire books devoted to the topic (Serravallo and Goldberg 2007). Conferring is even more important with your English learners because their language is developing at such a rapid rate. Some of the most difficult aspects of conferring are time, documentation, and deciding how to best use the precious time you have. Ideally, you should confer with all students at least once a week. I suggest this be done during their workshop and independent work time. I have also seen teachers do on-the-spot conferring sessions during small group.

The key to conferring is regularly meeting and checking in with students as indi-vidual learners. This time should be brief and used for an informal assessment about what the English learner is doing well and where she needs more support. Then, based on that information and previous data collected, you can use the majority of the time to coach the student with the exact instruction she needs. I structure my conferring sessions (and conferring notebook organization) in the following way:

1. Observe, discuss, and check in with student during independent work (read-ing, writing, responding, etc.).
2. Document and share something that is going well.
3. Provide coaching for an area of need or aspect of language support.
4. Encourage continued use in independent work.

I also use conferring to help me think about future needs-based small-group instruc-tion to target the specific needs of my English learners. For example, if I notice five of my English learners reading fluently but not stopping and fixing miscues when they alter the meaning of the text, I might pull a group to work on comprehension-monitoring strategies. Similarly, I also look specifically for their language development. I look at my notes from the previous conferring session to see what they were doing well and some language miscues I noticed. I use a classroom binder with tabs for each student for the conferring notebook. For each student, I attempt to document the following areas during conferring sessions (sometimes, I only get to one or two): general obser-vations, reading strengths, reading needs, language strengths, language needs, coach-ing focus for the session. This format allows me to target both language and reading needs—they are similar and interrelated, but they also often require different sup-ports and instruction for English learners than monolingual speakers. Figure 3.5 is a picture of Rachel Frevert conferring with her second-grade bilingual student about reading informational texts in English.

Figure 3.5
Conferring

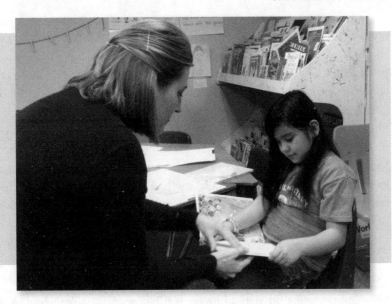

■ Assessment

Assessment for each of the individual reading workshop components (anchor lessons, guided learning experiences/workshop time, small group/word work, and reflection/ sharing) is addressed in detail in Chapters Four, Five, Six, and Seven. Much of that assessment will constitute how you assess your students over the course of a unit of study. However, it is also important to plan for both formative and summative assessments for both content and language objectives for English learners. As I plan my units of study, I consider ways I will assess whole-group, small-group, and independent work on a daily basis. Typically, this includes observations of independent reading and conversations about text as well as analyzing or grading student work (reading responses, written responses, inquiry projects, poems, etc.). During these informal assessments, try to consider *both* reading and language acquisition for your English learners. For a general understanding, you can simply assess students' progress toward the content and language objectives of the unit. They can be assessed using observations and documents from whole-group, small-group, and independent work and evaluation of the culminating event.

Although I find the ongoing, formative assessment to be the most useful in guiding my daily instruction, many teachers are required to provide more consistent and concrete evidence as assessment. Teacher-created rubrics and/or checklists based on the unit of study plan can be used to document student progress in a more formal way. However, these often leave out language acquisition considerations. I recommend creating an additional category to document the progression of language proficiency through the stages of language. A chart of the general stages of language proficiency is provided in Chapter One, but I have also seen teachers use a more detailed language acquisition chart to document progress. One teacher simply printed out copies of the language proficiency chart used for districtwide assessments for each English learner. She documented the date(s) where she observed the characteristic or behavior right on the chart over the course of the unit of study. She used this information not only for documentation but also as a guide for her one-on-one coaching and small-group instruction. By the end of the unit, she had evidence of her English learners' language progression and current stages of language proficiency. This information helped guide her planning for the next unit of study.

In Figure 3.6, you can see how I adapted the WIDA Can Do Descriptors to become an informal assessment about observed language development (WIDA provides extensive information about WIDA English Language Proficiency Standards and resources for supporting English learners at www.wida.us). This was used during an author unit of study. Notice how I documented the dates I observed Armando independently demonstrating the language characteristics as well as when I observed him demonstrating it with support (during conferring or small-group instruction). At the end of the unit, I noted his strong Developing stage characteristics followed by instructional needs that I wanted to use to support him in the following unit.

The key to assessment is guiding instruction. You have to decide what you want to know/assess about your students (please don't forget language acquisition!). Then, you can make informed instructional decisions to efficiently and effectively enhance reading and language development among your English learners.

AUTHOR STUDY UNIT   ARMANDO

Figure 5M: CAN DO Descriptors for the Levels of English Language Proficiency, PreK-12

For the given level of English language proficiency, **with support**, English language learners can:

	Level 1 Entering	Level 2 Beginning	Level 3 Developing	Level 4 Expanding	Level 5 Bridging	Level 6 Reaching
LISTENING	• Point to stated pictures, words, phrases • Follow one-step oral directions • Match oral statements to objects, figures or illustrations	• Sort pictures, objects according to oral instructions • Follow two-step oral directions • Match information from oral descriptions to objects, illustrations	• Locate, select, order information from oral descriptions • Follow multi-step oral directions [IN - 9|12,13,15] • Categorize or sequence oral information using pictures, objects	• Compare/contrast functions, relationships from oral information • Analyze and apply oral information • Identify cause and effect from oral discourse	• Draw conclusions from oral information • Construct models based on oral discourse • Make connections from oral discourse	
SPEAKING	• Name objects, people, pictures • Answer WH- (who, what, when, where, which) questions	• Ask WH- questions • Describe pictures, events, objects, people [IN - 9|15] • Restate facts	• Formulate hypotheses, make predictions [WS-9|17] • Describe processes, procedures • Retell stories or events [IN - 9|13,14,19]	• Discuss stories, issues, concepts • Give speeches, oral reports • Offer creative solutions to issues, problems	• Engage in debates • Explain phenomena, give examples and justify responses • Express and defend points of view	
READING	• Match icons and symbols to words, phrases or environmental print • Identify concepts about print and text features	• Locate and classify information • Identify facts and explicit messages • Select language patterns associated with facts	• Sequence pictures, events, processes [WS-9|9 IN-] • Identify main ideas [9|12,15] • Use context clues to [WS-IN-9|14,15] determine meaning of words [WS-9|15 IN-9|14,19,20]	• Interpret information or data • Find details that support main ideas • Identify word families [WS-9|16] figures of speech [IN-9|14]	• Conduct research to glean information from multiple sources • Draw conclusions from explicit and implicit text	
WRITING	• Label objects, pictures, diagrams • Draw in response to a prompt • Produce icons, symbols, words, phrases to convey messages	• Make lists • Produce drawings, phrases, short sentences, notes [IN - 9|19] • Give information requested from oral or written directions	• Produce bare-bones expository or narrative texts • Compare/contrast information [WS- 9|15] • Describe events, people, processes, procedures [WS-9|13 IN-9|15]	• Summarize information from graphics or notes • Edit and revise writing • Create original ideas or detailed responses	• Apply information to new contexts • React to multiple genres and discourses • Author multiple forms/ genres of writing	

Variability of students' cognitive development due to age, grade level spans, their diversity of educational experiences and diagnosed learning disabilities (if applicable) are to be considered in using this information.

IN = INDEPENDENT USE
WS = WITH SUPPORT

*Strong Developing characteristics
Next Steps - Need more opportunities for
     speaking + listening interpretations
- Introduce + support
- Need stronger writing connections

Figure 3.6 *Informal Assessment*

Resource Guide

Reflection

☐ Brainstorm possible units of study appropriate for your grade level. What differentiation considerations will be most important for supporting a wide range of language proficiency levels in your classroom units of study?

☐ Reflect on your current balance of fiction versus informational text. How could you work toward a more even balance?

☐ Consider one informational, one fictional, and one poetry unit of study that would work in your grade level. What mini-lessons and learning experiences would be crucial to your English learners' success throughout the unit?

☐ How will you plan, organize, and manage whole-group, small-group, and independent work and conferring sessions? Create a system for planning and documenting these essential components.

☐ How will you assess language and literacy progress for your English learners throughout each of the previously mentioned units of study?

CHAPTER 4

Whole-Group Anchor Lessons with Read-Alouds

"**M**Y STUDENTS NEED MORE EXPLICIT INSTRUCTION THAN A WORKSHOP provides. My students can't just be independently reading books of their choice. How do I demonstrate ideas and skills? How can I ensure I am meeting the needs of all my students?" I heard this from a teacher before I was about to start a professional development workshop on supporting the needs of diverse learners in the reading workshop. I completely understood her panic because I remember the same feeling when I began moving away from the district-mandated, teacher-centered curriculum. It felt intimidating to me for a couple of reasons: (1) I worried if I strayed from the curriculum, I would be blamed for students who continued to struggle to demonstrate "proficiency" on standardized assessments. (2) The curriculum was aligned with all of the standards. (3) The curriculum was already there and published, so I figured people who knew more than I did must have created it. These were all fears I had along with the misconception that there is little to no explicit whole-group instruction in a reading workshop.

I quickly realized the role of the teacher is even more crucial in student-centered curriculum because the teacher is responsible for facilitating meaningful whole-group, small-group, and individual reading experiences. Yes, students need to have choice and read independently (more on that in Chapter Five), but they also need purpose-ful anchor lessons with explicit content and language objectives for their reading in all contexts (independent, small-group, whole-group, in and out of school) to be more meaningful. My fear subsided as I realized no one knew my students better than I did, and because of that, I could provide meaningful instruction that aligned with the standards, prepared my students for internal and external assessments, and do a better job of supporting my students who were still working toward "proficiency" than a commercially produced reading program. So, I told the teacher I understood her concerns and that we were going to discuss ways to provide purposeful whole-group, small-group, and individualized instruction, starting with whole-group anchor lessons.

Broad Overview: What is it? Why do we do it? How do we plan for it?

An anchor lesson (in my classroom) is a lesson that grounds the students in deeper thinking, discussion, exploration, and engagement with literature in the unit of study. I think of anchor lessons as the heart or anchor of introducing and mentoring students in the larger context of literacy development. They are introductions to ways of thinking, talking, exploring, and experiencing literature. Although minilessons on comprehension strategies, word work, fluency, and so on are valuable (and will be addressed in Chapter Six), anchor lessons build community and a continuity of language surrounding essential skills for meaning making, critical thinking, and ways of interacting with texts. They are situated in the context of the Gradual Release of Responsibility Model (Pearson and Gallagher 1983) in that they include a demonstration or modeling by the teacher, followed by guided practice, collaborative work, and independent practice.

Anchor lessons are whole-group lessons with a shared literary experience involving a read-aloud. As Serafini (2006) explains, "What occurs during reading aloud and discussing literature affects how individuals transact with texts independently . . . How literature is discussed during the read-aloud provides the most concrete demonstration of the ways we want students to read and think on their own and in small groups" (22). Reading aloud to children has been documented to enhance their ability to use spoken English (Cohen 1968), increase vocabulary development (Ulanoff and Pucci 1999), and improve reading comprehension (Dickenson and Smith 1994).

Don't be mistaken, simply reading aloud to children is not enough and does not qualify as an anchor lesson. Additionally, the read-aloud/shared literary experience does not always need to be a picture book; some read-alouds might involve student writing, song lyrics, poetry, newspaper articles, and so on. The read-alouds in anchor lessons involve purposeful and interactive instruction building on the sharing of ideas. The sharing of ideas in this context moves beyond literal recall and comprehension questions; instead students should be encouraged to question, analyze, and interpret the texts. As we all know, this does not just magically happen, hence the need for the modeling, guided practice, collaboration, and independent practice grounded in the objectives of the anchor lesson.

In multilingual classrooms, anchor lessons with read-alouds also provide an opportunity for interactions with focused content and language skills and opportunities for differentiation. Multiple scholars have reported the benefits of reading aloud to English learners (Drucker 2003; Freeman and Freeman 2000). The read-alouds and accompanying instruction have been documented to improve both vocabulary and comprehension for English learners (Hickman, Pollard-Durodola, and Vaughn 2004). Although teachers tend to read aloud more fiction than informational texts, informational texts provide opportunities to draw on young bilinguals' background knowledge about the world around them while simultaneously developing vocabulary. Engagement with this type of text has been documented to motivate young learners and encourage overall literacy development (Caswell and Duke 1998). Researchers have reported substantial benefits of increased exposure, access, and knowledge about informational texts (Pappas 1991; Purcell-Gates, Duke, and Martineau 2007).

■ Specific Ideas for Instruction (Fiction and Informational Focus)

In the following sections, I include sample anchor lessons including the unit focus, content and language objectives of the anchor lesson, cornerstone text, teaching procedures, vignettes from the multilingual classrooms, and samples of English learners' work and interactions. I provide suggestions for differentiation according to stages of language proficiency, address ways to assess students, and provide children's literature suggestions for both primary and intermediate classrooms. In this chapter, I share a primary lesson with an informational text focus and an intermediate lesson with a fictional text focus.

Primary Anchor Lesson (Informational Text)

Unit Focus

Researching natural disasters

Content Objectives

☐ I can research a natural disaster.

☐ I can identify two nonfiction text features and their purpose.

Language Objectives

☐ I can listen to information about a natural disaster.

☐ I can share information I learned with others.

☐ I can use two nonfiction text features in my research.

Cornerstone Text

Volcano: The Eruption and Healing of Mount St. Helens (Lauber 1986)

Anchor Lesson Teaching Procedures

1. Select a quality informational text with multiple examples of the nonfiction text feature(s) you wish to address.
2. Utilize a document camera or prepare an enlarged version of an image with labels and a caption (alter this according to your text feature focus).
3. Choral read (or read aloud) the content and language objectives.
4. Introduce important vocabulary with supporting images to build background.
5. Read aloud, drawing attention to and asking students what they notice about the nonfiction text features.
6. Name the nonfiction text feature and create a chart with purposes for using the nonfiction text feature and examples.
7. Continue reading and continue adding to the chart. The following are some possible ideas for selection: title, heading, bold words, image, cutaways labels, captions, diagram, table.
8. Ask students to select a natural disaster of their choice to research.
9. After reading about their natural disaster, have students represent a new understanding utilizing an image, label, and caption (or the nonfiction text features you have introduced) and share in a small-group setting.
10. Revisit the content and language objectives.

Stories from the Classroom

I had the opportunity to model some lessons and team-teach in a second-grade bilingual classroom where students received the majority of their instruction in their first language (Spanish). During their English as a second language block, we combined instruction surrounding science content found in nonfiction texts and academic language support through scaffolded English instruction. So, I was teaching in English (with many language supports) to Spanish speakers who were reading, writing, and learning new science content in their second language, English.

I held up the cover of the book *Volcano: The Eruption and Healing of Mount St. Helens* (Lauber 1986) and told students we were going to be learning more about volcanoes (I pointed to the volcano on the cover as I said the word to provide additional visual support for the English learners) and other natural disasters. I explained that we were going to learn what caused volcanoes (again pointing at the image) and what happened after they erupted. Prior to the lesson, I had copied, enlarged, and laminated a volcano cutaway image. I also made labels with an accompanying image on sentence strips. The image next to the vocabulary word/label matched the images in the cutaway (just smaller). I told the students that these were important vocabulary words we were going to encounter during our reading that would help us understand volcanoes. I invited the students to choral read the vocabulary word with me as I taped it on the enlarged volcano cutaway.

Using the cutaway, I explained that the Earth's crust is a layer called the *mantle*, which is made up of plates that are always moving and shifting (I pointed to the labels of *mantle* and *plates*). I used my hands to gesture/model shifting plates and then colliding plates as I explained that sometimes the plates collide and one plate can slide under the other. I pointed to the *magma* label and explained that it collects under the Earth. If the pressure is high enough or a crack opens in the crust, the magma spews out (I motioned the movement with my hands and the image). I told them it is then called *lava* (I pointed to the *lava* image and label). Then, I asked students to look at the cover of the book again and tell someone next to them what they noticed. Many students began with using the word *volcano*, but other students used some of the new vocabulary words (*lava* was the most popular).

I modeled a read-aloud of the first section of the text. I made sure to emphasize and point out the vocabulary words and refer back to our image and vocabulary labels. During the read-aloud, I formally introduced the nonfiction text features of labels and captions and emphasized the amount of information that could be gained from utilizing the images as a complement to the printed text (the labels, captions, and body). I asked students to discuss the purpose of the nonfiction text features in the example that included the image, labels, and caption. Jorge commented, "The picture helps us know what you are reading." Sarai said, "The labels tell us the important words and parts in the picture, and the caption tells what is in the picture." We started the chart (which we added to and refined over the next couple of weeks) that can be seen in Figure 4.1.

We continued reading, identified additional examples, and added to our nonfiction text features chart. Then, I asked students to self-select a natural disaster to research that interested them (earthquakes, hurricanes, tornadoes, etc.). Boxes of informational texts on the different natural disasters were accessible for students to peruse before making their selection. They had the choice to read independently or with other students in their natural disaster group. After reading about their natural disaster, I asked students to represent a new understanding utilizing an image, label, and caption. This provided the anchor lesson for reading and representing research. Students utilized these skills during independent reading and writing time, and I used them as a foundation from which to continue building knowledge and skills in relation to reading and representing research.

Nonfiction Text Feature	Purpose	Example
Images	"Help us to know what you are reading."—Jorge "Show us what is hard to understand from just words."—Chris	Sketched example
Labels	"Tell us the important words and parts in the picture."—Sarai "It's like the vocabulary words."—Jon	Added labels with arrows to image
Captions	"Tell what is in the picture."—Sarai "It's the story of the picture, so we know what's going on."—Paloma	Added caption below image with labels

Figure 4.1 *Nonfiction Text Features Chart*

Differentiation and Considerations According to Proficiency Levels

Stages of Language Proficiency	Teacher Roles	English Learner Expectations/Performance
STAGE 1: *Preproduction* *Silent Period* *(Starting)*	☐ Use slowed speech and emphasize vocabulary by pointing to, gesturing, and repeating essential words during the read-aloud, nonfiction text features chart creation, and guided practice. ☐ Read aloud or have a peer read aloud to students. ☐ When possible, pair the student with a classmate who speaks the student's first language. ☐ When conferencing with stage 1 students, focus only on image with the possibility of a copied one- to two-word label.	☐ Will most likely be unable to choral read the objectives. ☐ After modeling of image text feature, English learners should be able to point to images. ☐ Can listen to teacher or partner read aloud. ☐ Can copy or create images. ☐ Can use first language to label or name images. ☐ May be able to copy image and brief label.
STAGE 2: *Early Production* *(Emerging)*	☐ Read aloud or have a peer read aloud to students. ☐ Encourage students to document understanding in first and second language when possible with labels and/or captions. ☐ Provide sentence starters for captions. Example: This is a picture of _____. ☐ When conferencing with stage 2 students, focus on image and simple copied labels. Scribe captions when possible and encourage rehearsal and sharing with peers.	☐ Might be able to choral read parts of the objectives. ☐ After modeling of text features, can point to images, labels, and captions. ☐ Can copy or create images with simple labels. ☐ Can attempt to fill in the blank and/or copy the sentence starter. ☐ Can share simple labels or a brief copied or scribed caption in partners or small groups after having a chance to practice/rehearse. (See Figure 4.2.)
STAGE 3: *Speech Emergence* *(Developing)*	☐ Have students participate in a paired reading and discussion about nonfiction text features prior to creating their image, label, and caption. ☐ Encourage students to create an image and label (in English). ☐ Ask students to write a caption using the sentence starter provided. ☐ Encourage students to share a nonfiction text feature example and purpose with a partner before sharing with the class.	☐ Can choral read objectives. ☐ Can participate in a partner reading of nonfiction text (appropriate level). ☐ Can identify and replicate image, label, and caption (using sentence starter). ☐ Can share learning and image, label, and caption with small or whole group after having a chance to practice/rehearse.

(continues)

Stages of Language Proficiency (continued)	Teacher Roles	English Learner Expectations/Performance
STAGE 4: *Intermediate Fluency (Expanding)*	☐ Have students participate in paired or independent reading. ☐ Encourage discussion about nonfiction text features prior to independent practice. ☐ Ask students to create an image with 2–5 labels. The caption from their learning should be in their own words, not copied from the text (summarize their learning). ☐ Encourage students to discuss and share with partners, small group, and whole class.	☐ Can choral read objectives. ☐ Can participate in independent or paired reading of grade-level nonfiction texts. ☐ Can identify examples and purpose of image, labels, and captions. ☐ Can document new learning by creating an image with 2–5 labels and a self-created caption. ☐ Can share writing and thinking with classmates. (See Figure 4.3.)
STAGE 5: *Advanced Fluency (Bridging)*	☐ Encourage students to move beyond initial instruction and modeling by providing the image, labels, and captions in their own words, identifying difficult vocabulary with accompanying explanations, and discussing possible consequences of natural disasters.	☐ Can choral read objectives. ☐ Can identify examples and purpose of image labels and captions. ☐ Can document new learning with self-created image, labels, captions, and summaries. ☐ Can identify and define difficult vocabulary. ☐ Can discuss possible consequences of natural disasters. (See Figure 4.4.)

I have included three images of student examples from Rachel Busetti Frevert's classroom. Figures 4.2 and 4.3 include bilingual second graders' illustration, labels and captions of a volcano and tornado. Figure 4.4 includes an illustration with labels and a brief summary written in the student's own words.

Children's Literature Suggestions (Primary)

Bauer, Marion Dane. 2008. *Flood!* Washington, D.C.: National Geographic Kids.

Goin, Miriam Busch. 2009. *Storms.* Washington, D.C.: National Geographic Kids.

Lauber, Patricia. 1986. *Volcano: The Eruption and Healing of Mount St. Helens.* New York: Aladdin.

Prager, Ellen J. 2007. *Volcano!* Washington, D.C.: National Geographic Kids.

———. 2007. *Earthquakes.* Washington, D.C.: National Geographic Kids.

Children's Literature Suggestions (Intermediate)

Challoner, Jack. 2004. *Hurricane and Tornado.* New York: DK Publishing.

Davis, Graeme. 2012. *Floods.* North Mankato, MN: Cherry Lake Publishing.

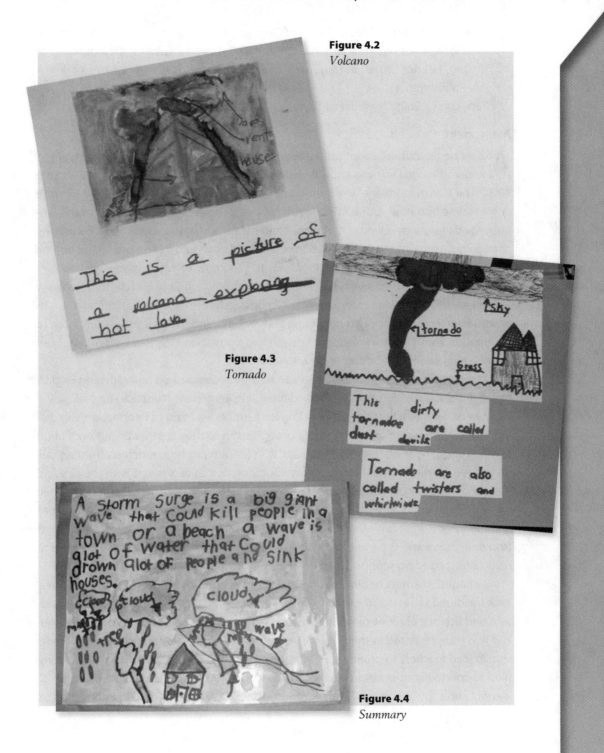

Figure 4.2
Volcano

Figure 4.3
Tornado

Figure 4.4
Summary

Grace, Catherine O'Neill. *Forces of Nature: The Awesome Power of Volcanoes, Earthquakes, and Tornados.* Washington, D.C.: National Geographic Kids.

Griffey, Harriet. 2010. *Earthquakes and Other Natural Disasters.* New York: DK Publishing.

Park, Louise. 2008. *Tornadoes.* Mankato, MN: Black Rabbit Books.

Assessment

As we begin to think about assessment we should ask ourselves, "What do I want to know? Why do I want to know it? How can I best discover it?" (Opitz and Guccione 2009). The formal language acquisition and literacy assessments can give us a glimpse or a baseline into how your English learners were performing on that day, but the language and literacy development of these students can change at a rapid rate. Formative, or ongoing, assessment provides vital information that should inform our instruction on a daily basis. For this particular lesson, I wanted to know to what degree we had met (or failed to meet) the following lesson objectives (both language and content) to know where I needed to provide more or less scaffolding in future lessons: I can research a natural disaster; I can identify two nonfiction text features and their purpose; I can listen to information about a natural disaster; I can share information I learned with others; I can use two nonfiction text features in my research.

Assessing these types of objectives can best be accomplished by examining English learners' work, observing discussions, and providing immediate feedback and scaffolding when necessary. Teachers can observe English learners listening to information, discussing, and contributing during the whole-group lesson as they are identifying nonfiction text features. These observations can assist in identifying how much scaffolding will be needed during the read-aloud and guided practice. In alignment with the Gradual Release of Responsibility Model (Pearson and Gallagher 1983), English learners can then work independently or with peers in their self-selected interest groups. This provides another opportunity for informal assessment of students as they select and read texts (some silently, some in partners or triads), and teachers can periodically ask students to read aloud, providing support when needed.

As English learners begin creating their representations utilizing the text features, look for demonstration of content understanding related to both the science content and literacy content of nonfiction text features. What was their natural disaster, and was it represented in their image, label, and caption? These informal assessments should lead teachers to provide some on-the-spot differentiated instruction. For example, I supported Starting and Emerging students by modeling and encouraging them to identify and copy important vocabulary and labels. I also encouraged Bridging students to provide information in their own words, providing an explanation of vocabulary and possible consequences of natural disasters (see Figure 4.4). Teachers can adjust their on-the-spot differentiation based on their observations and objectives. These assessments and differentiation should guide thinking about the next minilesson, differentiation and scaffolding.

Intermediate Anchor Lesson (Perspective and Bias)

Unit Focus
Identifying perspective and bias

Content Objective
☐ I can identify stereotypes.

Language Objectives
☐ I can read the story and share evidence supporting my interpretations of stereotypes.

☐ I can identify/code the supporting evidence as text-based, image-based, or both.

Cornerstone Text
Walt Disney's Cinderella (RH Disney 2005)

Anchor Lesson Teaching Procedures

1. Bring the students together for a read-aloud and show them the cover of *Walt Disney's Cinderella* (RH Disney 2005).
2. Explain that although many of them might be familiar with this story, you are going to read this story today looking for stereotypes. Explain that you are going to be looking for how the author and illustrator portray women and men in this story. Ask students to help you brainstorm on two charts the typical stereotypes of males and females.
3. Have students choral read the objectives aloud with you.
4. Share the following questions aloud and on a document camera or overhead to have students be thinking about the read-aloud:
   a. How do the author and illustrator present the women and men?
   b. What male and female stereotypes are in the story?
   c. What roles are they assigned? (Example: Women are mothers and care takers, vs. princes are providers and dragon slayers)
   d. If the female character was a male, how would it change the story?

5. Explain that these questions will help them analyze the perspective of the author and illustrator as they look for stereotypes. They will be paying attention to the roles of men and women with particular attention to male perspectives on gender and power.

6. Give students sticky notes to jot down evidence related to questions a, b, and c while you read the story aloud.

7. After reading the story, put up three pieces of chart paper (one for questions a, b, c), and ask students to turn and talk about their ideas in response to the questions. Ask for volunteers to share their ideas as you scribe them on the chart paper.

8. Have students add their sticky notes under the written responses that correspond with their evidence.

9. Read through the ideas and evidence together while asking students to help you code the evidence sticky notes as text-based (TB), image-based (IB), or both (B).

10. Ask students to turn and talk about the following question (d): If the female character was a male, how would it change the story? Then, discuss as a whole class.

11. Split the class into two groups—one will be reading and analyzing *The Paperbag Princess* (Munsch 1980) and the other will be reading and analyzing *Prince Cinders* (Cole 1997). Ask the students to replicate the critique with *Cinderella* in their groups and post written instructions to remind them of the procedure (charts with questions a, b, c; supporting evidence; coded evidence; and discussion from step 10).

12. Share out with the other group.

13. Revisit content and language objectives.

Stories from the Classroom

I was working in an urban fifth-grade classroom with twenty-eight students who received all of their instruction in English. Sixteen of the students spoke a language other than English at home, but only six of those students spoke Spanish; the other languages included Hmong, Korean, Portuguese, and Vietnamese. We had seen many students demonstrate signs of disengagement with independent-level texts that were not facilitating meaningful, age-appropriate, or critical conversations, so I selected picture books that could be used with a critical analysis to introduce perspective and bias.

"Miss, that's a baby book!" Angel shouted the second I pulled out the *Cinderella* book. The students began talking and agreeing that it was a "babyish princess" book. I quickly explained we were going to be analyzing and critiquing this text to see what kind of "grown-up" stereotypes and biases the book was presenting to the readers, many of whom are young children who enjoy what they called "babyish princess" stories. I told them we were going to reread this story with a gender stereotype lens, meaning that we were going to try to see how the author portrayed women and men. I explained that sometimes these things are hidden, but it is our job to be critical readers to find the bias and stereotypes, so we would be on the lookout for evidence of this during the read-aloud. I asked the students to choral read the content and language objectives with me.

Students helped me brainstorm stereotypes of males and females that included the following for males: they are strong; they are brave; they save the woman. The students generated more stereotype suggestions for women: they are pretty; they are mothers; they are nice; they are weak/need help from a man; they fall in love; they have "girl" jobs (when questioned about this, the student said, "You know, like they aren't doctors or police. They are like you—like teachers or moms"). I told them to keep these stereotypes in mind because we were going to analyze how women and men are portrayed in this story. I put the questions from the previous list on the document camera, read them aloud, and told students I wanted them to keep these questions in mind while I read aloud. I passed out sticky notes and asked students to document evidence that might support their reactions to the first three questions.

I read the story slowly, giving plenty of time for English learners to process the familiar story, view the illustrations, and write down their thinking and evidence. I then put up chart paper for each of the questions and asked students to share their thinking with peers first and then the group. They said things like, "She is pretty so he marries her and saves her" and "Cinderella is just cooking and cleaning, and all of them are trying to be pretty for the prince." After scribing their comments under each question, I asked for volunteers to add their evidence and we coded it (TB, IB, or B). I asked them how the story would be different if the males and females were reversed, and they all laughed. One English learner explained, "That just isn't how stories go." Another student said, "Katniss saved Peeta!" (referring to *The Hunger Games*). We talked about why women and men are portrayed in such stereotypical ways.

Then, I asked them to break into groups and do a feminist criticism on two "different" fairy tales, *The Paperbag Princess* and *Prince Cinders*. The students found the positioning of men and women in these tales entertaining. Their responses and analysis were quite different as they discussed how the men were now the ones taking on the "princess" roles. They shared out the analysis and coded supporting evidence with the other group. "The prince is weak. The paperbag princess saved him." They cited evidence from the picture and text where the princess outsmarted the dragon and saved the prince. They discussed that the stereotypes in these texts were the opposite of what we read about in *Cinderella*. I told students they would continue to read critically and analyze their reading for stereotypes and biases—not just gender, but also wealth, race, language, and arche-types such as hero, villain, fool, helper, and so on.

Differentiation and Considerations According to Proficiency Levels

Stages of Language Proficiency	Teacher Roles	English Learner Expectations/Performance
STAGE 1: *Preproduction Silent Period (Starting)*	☐ Use slowed speech and emphasize vocabulary by pointing to, gesturing, and repeating essential words during the read-aloud. ☐ Emphasize and refer back to image-based evidence to support comprehension. ☐ Allow students to work with a partner or respond with pictures on the sticky notes. ☐ Read aloud or have a peer read aloud to students during guided practice. ☐ When possible, pair the student with a classmate who speaks the student's first language. ☐ When conferencing with stage 1 students, focus only on image-based support for gender roles.	☐ Will most likely be unable to choral read the objectives. ☐ Can point to images of different gender roles. ☐ Can listen to teacher or partner read aloud. ☐ Might be able to create images on sticky notes with partners to document image-based support. ☐ Can use first language to label or name images.
STAGE 2: *Early Production (Emerging)*	☐ Read aloud or have a peer read aloud to students during guided practice. ☐ Provide time for turn and talk or partner discussions prior to sharing. ☐ Encourage students to document understanding in first and second language when possible with images and/or text. ☐ Provide sentence starters for responses on sticky notes. Example: The women in the story are _____. The men in the story are _____. The story would be different if the woman was a man because _____. ☐ When conferencing with stage 2 students, focus on image-based text. Scribe for students when possible and encourage rehearsal and sharing with peers.	☐ Might be able to choral read parts of the objectives. ☐ Can create images on sticky notes with partners to document image-based support. ☐ Can attempt to fill in the blank and/or copy the sentence starter with text or images. ☐ Can share language frame/sentence starter responses in partners or small groups after having a chance to practice/rehearse.

Stages of Language Proficiency *(continued)*	Teacher Roles	English Learner Expectations/Performance
STAGE 3: *Speech Emergence (Developing)*	☐ Have students participate in a small-group reading and discussion of gender bias and perspective. ☐ Encourage students to discuss their background knowledge about stereotypes. ☐ Ask students to write responses on sticky notes using the sentence starters provided. ☐ Encourage students to share their responses to questions with a partner before sharing with the class.	☐ Can choral read objectives. ☐ Can participate in a small-group reading and discussion of gender bias and perspective. ☐ Can create response sticky notes with partners to document image-based and text-based support. ☐ Can share language frame/sentence starter responses in partners or small groups after having a chance to practice/rehearse.
STAGE 4: *Intermediate Fluency (Expanding)*	☐ Have students participate in a small-group reading and discussion of gender bias and perspective. These students might lead or support the read-aloud and discussion in their small groups. ☐ Encourage students to discuss and connect their background knowledge about stereotypes. ☐ Ask students to write responses on sticky notes using their own words (moving away from the language frames). ☐ Encourage students to make connections to other texts and discuss and share with partners, small group, and whole class.	☐ Can choral read objectives. ☐ Can participate in and facilitate the read-aloud, analysis, and discussion of gender bias and perspective. ☐ Can create response sticky notes with partners to document image-based and text-based support. ☐ Can make connections across texts. ☐ Can share evidence-based responses in partners, small groups, and whole group after having a chance to practice/rehearse.
STAGE 5: *Advanced Fluency (Bridging)*	☐ Ask students to discuss and share the implications of such bias and perspective. ☐ Encourage students to move beyond initial instruction and modeling by using a different analytical lens to examine the same text (power, wealth, race, language, etc.).	☐ Can choral read objectives. ☐ Can participate in and facilitate the read-aloud, analysis, and discussion of gender bias and perspective. ☐ Can create response sticky notes with partners to document image-based and text-based support. ☐ Can make connections across texts. ☐ Can use additional analytical lenses. ☐ Can share evidence-based responses in partners, small groups, and whole group after having a chance to practice/rehearse. ☐ Can discuss implications of perspective and bias.

Children's Literature Suggestions (Primary)

Cole, Babette. 1997. *Princess Smartypants*. New York: Puffin.

DiPucchio, Kelly. 2012. *Grace for President*. New York: Hyperion Books.

Funke, Cornelia. 2004. *The Princess Knight*. New York: Chicken House.

———. 2007. *Princess Pigsty*. New York: Chicken House.

Willis, Jeanne. 2003. *I Want to Be a Cowgirl*. London: Andersen Press.

Children's Literature Suggestions (Intermediate)

Browne, Anthony. 1986. *Piggybook*. New York: Dragon Fly Books.

Cole, Babbette. 1997. *Prince Cinders*. New York: Puffin.

Disney Enterprises. 1998. *Cinderella*. New York: Golden Books Publishing.

Munsch, Robert. 1980. *The Paper Bag Princess*. New York: Annick Press.

Silverstein, Shel. 1964. *The Giving Tree*. New York: Harper Collins.

Assessment

Again, I asked myself, "What do I want to know? Why do I want to know it? How can I best discover it?" (Opitz and Guccione 2009). For this lesson on feminist criticism, I wanted to know to what degree we had met (or failed to meet) the following lesson objectives to guide my future instruction regarding the analysis of perspective and bias: I can identify stereotypes; I can read the story and share evidence supporting my interpretations of stereotypes; I can identify/code the supporting evidence as text-based, image-based, or both.

To best discover English learners' attainment of the objectives during the whole-group lesson, teachers can observe student discussions and sticky notes with evidence created by the students. This should help facilitate the remainder of the lesson by highlighting parts where some students needed more explicit explanation and/or supporting evidence. During the small-group reading and analysis, I recommend examining English learners' work and observing student discussions. During this time, teachers can provide immediate feedback and scaffolding when necessary, such as pointing to images and providing vocabulary support during discussion and writing on sticky notes. For example, I was able to observe students' working together to answer the feminist criticism question and find text-based and image-based evidence. Most of the students were highly engaged and contributed to the analysis on multiple levels. However, I also noticed during this time that there were three or four English learners who were not participating, even with prompting. I made a note to conference with these students the following day as they worked on a criticism during their independent reading.

Sometimes, the most informative assessment comes not when students are meeting the standards and objectives, but instead when teachers can identify that the students need more support. This is rarely a one-size-fits-all opportunity, so I recommend teachers utilize conferencing to identify more specific supports and immediate scaffolding that they can provide in a one-on-one setting with ongoing informal assessment. For example, teachers could support Starting and Emerging students with the use of language scaffolding, additional vocabulary support, and a couple language frames to help them respond to questions. These assessments and differentiation should help guide teachers' thinking about the next minilesson, differentiation, and scaffolding.

Reflection

- ☐ What type of content/skill/engagement instruction is currently included in your anchor lessons?
- ☐ What are some ideas for anchor lessons that build your classroom reading community by enhancing ways your students are engaging with text?
- ☐ How is your whole-group instruction supporting English learners' independent interactions with text?
- ☐ How can you enhance the focus and support in whole-group instruction for English learners? What specific language considerations and scaffolds might be most helpful at your grade level during whole-group instruction?
- ☐ How might you adapt the model lessons to fit with an upcoming unit you have planned?

CHAPTER 5

Guided Learning Experiences During Workshop Time

WITH A COHESIVE UNIT OF STUDY AND STRONG WHOLE-GROUP ANCHOR LESSONS in place, you can now provide specific and targeted differentiated instruction for English learners in small groups. However, the most common question I hear when working with teachers about getting their workshop up and running is, "What are all the other kids doing when I am working with a small group or conferring?" Although teachers of monolingual students also ask this question, it is a particularly pressing question for teachers of English learners. The following concerns seem to arise on a regular basis: "What about my newcomers who barely know any English, what will they do?" "What about my students who are not yet independently reading?" (With this question, teachers are often referring to decoding unfamiliar text without support.) "How will students be held accountable?" "What about the students who do not have the vocabulary necessary to comprehend the text without my support?" These are all important questions that must be considered when designing learning experiences for English learners when they are not with you. In many primary classrooms, it is common to have stations or centers during small-group time with activities or lessons students can do without the teacher. Unfortunately, these often become tedious tasks used to keep students busy so the teacher can provide small-group instruction without being interrupted.

In this chapter, I share options for guided learning experiences for English learners during the independent workshop time—in other words, learning opportunities created for English learners to engage in meaningful experiences with literature independently, in pairs, or in small groups without the teacher. I provide answers to the common concerns mentioned above by teachers in addition to sharing practical suggestions for differentiation according to proficiency levels.

Broad Overview: What is it? Why do we do it? How do we plan for it?

Like in a pottery studio, at this point the instructor has provided modeling, instruction, and guided practice with the anchor lessons, but now it is the emerging artists' turn to try it out in their own context. The instructor's role in guided learning experiences is to support independence. Guided learning experiences during the independent workshop time are more than SSR (sustained silent reading) or DEAR (drop everything and read). Although I appreciate and support these programs, workshop is a time for students to hone their craft of being readers. Guided learning experiences should provide an opportunity for readers to read, apply their learning and thinking to reading, and respond to reading in meaningful ways without the direct instruction of the teacher. These three components can be done in a multitude of ways ranging from silent reading with a reading response to dramatic arts to student-led book clubs or literature circles to independent responses to reading based on concepts and skills from anchor lessons. The options are endless, but there are two parameters to consider when planning that I have found make this time more successful: choice and accountability.

Choice

The first parameter is choice. English learners must have choice. This could be choice in text, choice in strategy use, choice in format (e.g., aloud, silent, with a partner), and/or choice in response (e.g., reading response, application of anchor lesson concepts, discussion). Again, this is good practice for teachers of monolingual students, but it provides additional benefits for English learners. The ability to select a text at their instructional level is largely dependent on their background knowledge and vocabulary. Research has shown that increased practice with materials at the independent level typically results in fluency and word recognition improvement

(Kame'enui and Simmons 2001). Giving students the option to select their own independent-level text allows English learners to find texts of interest with which they are able to build vocabulary by making connections from their prior knowledge to new learning.

The goal with choice for English learners (beyond the obvious benefits of motivation and engagement) is encouraging students to be metacognitive about their language and literacy development. They can select books that are accessible and assist in their language and literacy development, and they should also have the choice to select strategies that support their comprehension. I have seen many teachers assign a specific number of comprehension strategies during students' independent reading. For example, students will be asked to document two questions, two answers, and two connections during their reading. Unfortunately, this defeats the purpose of comprehension strategies. Comprehension strategies should be used to assist in comprehension, and strategy use varies from student to student and text to text. For example, in a yearlong study, I found viewing images to be the most frequently used strategy by first-grade English learners, followed by summarizing and documenting information they learned and interactive discussions (Guccione [Moses] 2011). Knowing this, teachers of English learners should present students with a choice of comprehension strategies while recognizing that some of the less frequently addressed strategies like viewing and interactive discussions with peers might be the most beneficial options for supporting comprehension of English learners.

The goal of workshop time for English learners is to read, think, learn, explore, and discuss. English learners can benefit from silent reading, reading with partners (Herrera, Perez, and Escamilla 2010), and language use with peers during collaborative projects and discussion (Hansen 1989; Gibbons 2002). Because of this, English learners should have options for how they want to read (silent or aloud) as well as how they would like to respond. Giving students a menu of options for responding to reading allows English learners to differentiate for themselves in terms of their expressive output. A sample menu will be provided for both informational and fiction texts in the instructional suggestions sections. Sentence stems with more formulaic responses or images with labels might be appropriate for speakers in the early stages of language proficiency, whereas critique and analysis or an argument-writing response might be more appropriate for students closer to the Bridging stage.

Accountability

Accountability is addressed in greater detail in the assessment section, but accountability is not just about assessment. Setting high expectations with predictable routines and outcomes fosters a structured workshop in which English learners can thrive. Even when giving students a menu of options for reading and responding, students need to be clear on the objectives. When initially introducing a menu option for their guided learning experiences, the teacher must model, provide guided practice, and make explicit what English learners should be able to do, know, and demonstrate by the end of their workshop time with any particular selection. See the example in Figure 5.1 from Rachel Busetti Frevert's classroom where students are working on inquiry projects about animals. In this image, she has posted and introduced the expectations for what students will be doing during workshop, why they will be doing it, and how they will know they have met expectations. Additional examples could include students submitting reading logs, reading responses, reflections from discussion groups, a summary of their reading, or self-assessment of their participation.

Specific Ideas for Instruction (Fiction and Informational Focus)

In the following sections, I include a menu of options for guided learning experiences during workshop time. Each section (fiction and informational) will include a sample anchor lesson that introduces the guided learning experience including the unit focus,

Figure 5.1
Goals and Expectations

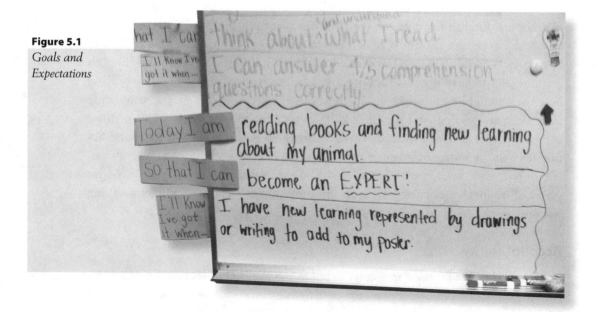

content and language objectives of the anchor lesson, cornerstone text, teaching procedures, vignettes from the classrooms, and samples of student work and interactions. I provide suggestions for differentiation according to stages of language proficiency, address ways to assess students, and provide children's literature suggestions for both primary and intermediate classrooms. Remember, the goal is fostering independence for meaningful literacy experiences for English learners without the teacher, but for that to take place, we must first model and provide guided practice. Once students can independently participate in the guided learning experience, you can add it to their menu of options for their workshop time while you are conferring or working with small groups. In this chapter, I share a primary lesson with a fiction text focus and an upper-elementary lesson with an informational text focus.

Primary Anchor Lesson to Introduce Guided Learning Experience: Author Study (Fiction Texts)

Unit Focus
Author study

Content Objectives
☐ I can summarize a book by Kevin Henkes.
☐ I can provide my opinion about the book.

Language Objectives
☐ I can read a book with a partner.
☐ I can write a reading response entry.
☐ I can create a visual representation for my reading response entry.

Cornerstone Text
Wemberly Worried (Henkes 2000)

Anchor Lesson Teaching Procedures

1. Select a quality- and age-appropriate fiction author for your author study unit.
2. Select the cornerstone text that you will read aloud to the students and use for modeling and guided practice for reading response options.
3. Utilize a document camera or prepare chart paper to resemble graphic organizer response formats, paper, or notebooks where your students will be writing their reading responses (for kindergarten, this is typically a large space for writing with one or two large penmanship lines for writing, whereas this is typically standard spiral notebooks for upper elementary). Include sections for an illustration, book title, author, illustrator, summary, and opinion. See Figure 5.2.

4. Choral read (or read aloud) the content and language objectives.
5. Tell students you will be reading a book by the featured author and as a class, you will be creating a reading response entry with information about the book, a summary, an illustration, and an opinion (show them the chart or graphic organizer).
6. Read aloud, stopping periodically and asking students to turn and talk about what has happened in the book and their thinking.
7. After finishing the book, direct students' attention to the whole-class reading response format. As you introduce each section, create a visual representation for the expected content (e.g., draw a book cover with an arrow to the title for the section where they have to write the title to help English learners with new academic vocabulary for the reading response).

Figure 5.2

Graphic Organizer

Book Title:

Author: Illustrator:

Characters:

Draw a picture of what happened in the beginning, middle and end of the story

Summary (What happened?):

Big Idea (What was the message or lesson)?

Opinion (What did you think?):

Full-size reproducible available at www.heinemann.com/products/E05757.aspx.

8. Ask students to turn and talk for each section before scribing their thinking onto the chart.

9. Explain that students are going to work with partners to read another book by the author and create their own reading response.

10. As students are reading and working together on reading responses, walk around the room to provide additional support as needed.

11. Share volunteer student examples and tell students this will be an option to add to the guided learning experiences during workshop time menu.

12. Revisit the content and language objectives.

Stories from the Classroom

I was teaching second grade in an English-instruction classroom in a bilingual elementary school. Approximately 75 percent of my students' first language was Spanish, and I also had one student whose first language was Hmong. I displayed many Kevin Henkes' books on the whiteboard railing and told students we were going to begin an author study on Kevin Henkes (we had completed other author studies, so they were familiar with the process). Many of them recognized the books and shared that they had seen or read them before. I introduced *Wemberly Worried* (Henkes 2000) for the cornerstone text and pointed at the words as I read the title and author. I told them we were going to be reading and learning a new way to respond to reading. Then, I asked them to choral read the content and language objectives with me.

Prior to the lesson, I created a poster-sized graphic organizer for the reading response as well as a smaller version for students' independent reading responses. I created visual representations for each section as well as a representative illustration for students' responses. For example, next to the word *title*, I sketched a cover of a book with an arrow pointing toward the title. I showed students the poster and explained that we would be creating a reading response entry with information about the book, a summary, an illustration, and an opinion. I read the title and author/illustrator information and then asked students to try to act out what it meant to be worried with a partner. Some students looked confused, so I asked an English learner who was acting it out to share his acting and thinking with the class. Julian said, "It's kinda like being scared. Like you think something bad is going to happen." I asked the students to try to act out being worried again with their partner and then began the read-aloud.

I modeled a read-aloud of the first section of the text. I made sure to emphasize and point out the images of vocabulary words I thought might be troublesome (like *worried*). During the read-aloud, I stopped twice to ask students to talk in partners about what had happened so far. Then, I asked the students to share their opinion and reactions to the book. I asked them to think about what they thought the "big idea" was or what the author was trying to tell or teach us. After the read-aloud and discussion, I encouraged them to help me fill out the reading response chart and add pictures to help us remember our thinking. When the chart was completed, I explained they would be working with a partner to read another Kevin Henkes' book and complete a reading response. I allowed students to self-select partners and books before returning to their seats with the reading response graphic organizers. Figure 5.2 is a sample graphic organizer that can be used for reading responses described in this classroom story.

I provided additional support when necessary while English learners were working in partners. Then, I called the group back to the rug and asked if any students would like to share their reading response with the rest of the class. After some student sharing, we choral read the objectives and students gave a thumbs up if they felt they had met the objective or a thumbs down if they did not. I reminded students that reading responses were now going to be an option during workshop time, so we needed to add it to our guided learning experiences menu (it was early in the year, so the other current options included reading to myself, reading with a partner, listening center, whisper reading, drawing and writing, word family poetry). A sample guided learning experiences menu for the end of a year in first grade might include the following options:

- independent and paired reading
- whisper reading
- big book pointer reading
- book club
- listening center
- author/illustrator studies
- literature study groups
- readers' theater
- poetry rehearsal and performance
- inquiry projects
- word work
- response experiences
  - » reading response options
  - » talk about texts
  - » read another connected text
  - » make suggestions for other readers/book talk
  - » sketch ideas about texts
  - » question the text/ideas
  - » reread text

» reflect in writing
» write to the author/illustrator
» use ideas for own writing

Students in my second-grade classroom utilized reading responses during independent reading and writing time, and I used them as a foundation to continue building knowledge and skills in relation to responding to reading. Some English learners took on more complex and open-ended formats and responses, and other students needed modifications and additional support. Figure 5.3 is an alternative option for a reading response with a sentence starter from Rachael Pritchard's multi-lingual first-grade classroom.

Figure 5.3
Reading Response

Differentiation and Considerations According to Proficiency Levels

Stages of Language Proficiency	Teacher Roles	English Learner Expectations/Performance
STAGE 1: *Preproduction Silent Period (Starting)*	☐ Use slowed speech and emphasize vocabulary by pointing to, gesturing, and repeating essential words during the read-aloud. ☐ Use visual images whenever possible to support understanding (pictures on the graphic organizer). Give graphic organizer with visual cues on it. ☐ Allow students to work with a partner and respond with pictures. ☐ Read aloud or have a peer read aloud to students during partner reading and response. ☐ When possible, pair the student with a classmate who speaks the student's first language. ☐ When conferencing with stage 1 students, focus only on basic title, author/illustrator, and possible image creation.	☐ Will mostly likely be unable to choral read the objectives. ☐ Can point to images. ☐ Can listen to teacher or partner read aloud. ☐ Might be able to copy the title, author/illustrator. ☐ Might be able to sketch images of beginning, middle, and end of the text after listening to peers read and viewing the illustrations.
STAGE 2: *Early Production (Emerging)*	☐ Use visual cues for graphic organizer. Give graphic organizer with visual cues on it. ☐ Read aloud or have a peer read aloud to students during partner reading and response. ☐ Encourage students to document understanding in first and second languages when possible with images and/or text. ☐ Provide sentence starters for responses on graphic organizer. Example: Wemberly was worried because _____. I liked the story because _____. I didn't like the story because _____. ☐ When conferencing with stage 2 students, focus on images and simple text. Scribe for students when possible and encourage sharing with peers.	☐ Might be able to choral read parts of the objectives. ☐ Can create images on graphic organizer with partners to document what happened in the story. ☐ Can attempt to fill in the blank and/or copy the sentence starter with text or images. ☐ Can share language frame/sentence starter responses in partners or small groups after having a chance to practice/rehearse.

Stages of Language Proficiency *(continued)*	Teacher Roles	English Learner Expectations/Performance
STAGE 3: *Speech Emergence (Developing)*	☐ Have students participate in a partner reading, graphic organizer completion, and discussion of the book. ☐ Encourage students to document understanding in English with images and text. ☐ Provide sentence starters for responses on graphic organizer. Example: Wemberly was worried because _____. ☐ The lesson in this story was _____. I liked the story because _____. I didn't like the story because _____. ☐ Encourage students to share their responses with a partner before sharing with the class.	☐ Can choral read objectives. ☐ Can participate in a partner reading and discussion of the book. ☐ Can complete the graphic organizer in English using images and text. ☐ Can share language frame/sentence starter responses for graphic organizer completion with partners, or whole group if they choose.
STAGE 4: *Intermediate Fluency (Expanding)*	☐ Have students participate in a partner reading, graphic organizer completion, and discussion of the book. ☐ Ask students to write responses on the graphic organizer using their own words (moving away from the language frames). ☐ Encourage students to make connections to other texts by Kevin Henkes; discuss and share with partners and whole class.	☐ Can choral read objectives. ☐ Can participate in and facilitate the read-aloud and completion of the reading response. ☐ Can create reading responses with partners to document understanding and reaction to the book. ☐ Can make connections across texts. ☐ Can share evidence-based responses with partners and whole group after having a chance to practice/rehearse with partners.
STAGE 5: *Advanced Fluency (Bridging)*	☐ Ask students to complete reading response using their own words. Ask students to use transitional words when creating a paragraph for the summary section. ☐ Encourage students to move beyond initial instruction and modeling by creating a Venn diagram to compare two Kevin Henkes' texts. ☐ Ask students to identify characteristics of Kevin Henkes' writing that they see in both texts.	☐ Can participate in and facilitate the read-aloud and completion of the reading response. ☐ Can create reading responses with partners to document understanding and reaction to the book. ☐ Can identify similarities and differences between two texts written by the same author. ☐ Can identify characteristics of an author's writing. ☐ Can share evidence-based responses in partners and whole group.

Children's Literature Suggestions (Primary)

Books by Kevin Henkes

1987. *Sheila Rae, the Brave*. New York: Greenwillow.

1991. *Chrysanthemum*. New York: Greenwillow.

1993. *Owen*. New York: Greenwillow.

1996. *Lilly's Purple Plastic Purse*. New York: Greenwillow.

2000. *Wemberly Worried*. New York: Greenwillow.

2001. *Sheila Rae's Peppermint Stick*. New York: Greenwillow.

2002. *Owen's Marshmallow Chick*. New York: Greenwillow.

2003. *Wemberly's Ice-Cream Star*. New York: Greenwillow.

2006. *Lilly's Big Day*. New York: Greenwillow.

2012. *Penny and Her Song*. New York: Greenwillow.

2013. *Penny and Her Marble*. New York: Greenwillow.

Children's Literature Suggestions (Intermediate)

Books by Anthony Browne

1977. *Through the Magic Mirror*. New York: Greenwillow Books.

1977. *A Walk in the Park*. London: Hamish Hamilton Children's Books.

1983. *Gorilla*. London: Julia MacRae Books.

1986. *Piggybook*. New York: Alfred A. Knopf.

1990. *Changes*. London: Julia MacRae.

1991. *Willy's Pictures*. Cambridge, MA: Candlewick.

1992. *Zoo*. New York: Knopf.

1997. *The Tunnel*. London: Walker Books.

1998. *Voices in the Park*. New York: DK Publishers.

Assessment

When assessing students, we have to return to examining what teachers want to know about their English learners, and we need to consider the most effective ways of discovering that information. During guided learning experiences, there are often three things teachers want to know: (1) Were the students on task and did they use their time for academic purposes? (2) How were the students using and applying their knowledge? Did we meet the objectives? (3) Where do they need additional instruction and support? Next, I address why those questions are important and how teachers can best discover it.

QUESTION 1: Were the students on task and did they use their time for academic purposes?

This is typically what teachers want to know first because they want valuable learning and practice to take place for all students even when they are working with other students. Teachers can discover and assess students' use of time in multiple ways. The first and most obvious way is observation—teachers have a pretty good idea when students are not using their independent work time to work. Beyond the observations, accountability measures can help teachers discover how students were using their time. I have seen this done in multiple ways. Collecting reading response notebooks and/or other expressive products students are working on from the menu will give you an idea of what they were practicing and learning without you. I have also seen teachers give students self-evaluation rubrics to reflect on their accomplishments and behavior during independent work time. One teacher who was having particular difficulty with this question had students jot down their goal and objective for independent work time in their reading response journal and share it with a partner. At the end of the independent work period, students rated themselves and their partner on whether or not the goal was accomplished. Then, based on that, they set a goal for what they would be working on the following day.

QUESTION 2: How were the students using and applying their knowledge? Did we meet the objectives?

As with most assessments, observation is always a valuable tool. Observing students "practicing" options for guided learning experiences during workshop time before you actually start working with small groups or conferring can be a huge help. As students are working in small groups, pairs or individually, you can provide the necessary scaffolding and feedback to support their independence. For example, this would be a time to confer with students at different levels of language proficiency to suggest adaptations or differentiation options after observing how they are using and applying their knowledge (suggested alterations mentioned in the language proficiency chart).

Additionally, you can collect their reading responses. This will give you a more in-depth look at their expressive output in English when responding to literature without your support. You can assess both content applications (such as summarizing, comprehension, etc.) as well as language development (ways English learners are using and approximating English in their written responses).

QUESTION 3: Where do they need additional instruction and support?

For me, this is the most important assessment question. Observation and analysis of their reading responses should be used to guide future instruction. As you listen to English learners read and discuss literature with peers, consider areas of instruction related to both second language and literacy skill development. When you are working with other students and cannot observe, their reading responses (or other menu options) can provide a window into their thinking and application of skills being used independently. Use this as an opportunity to identify things they are doing well and areas they could use additional support. During your small-group time, you can then use this information to provide targeted instruction for language support as well as literacy skills such as decoding and comprehension.

Intermediate Anchor Lesson to Introduce Guided Learning Experience: Independent Inquiry (Informational Text)

This lesson assumes the students have already been exposed to the research process with a specific topic (like the natural disasters example, not an independent inquiry), informational text features, and their purposes. If you are introducing this for the first time, refer to the informational anchor lesson in the previous chapter and adjust according to your grade level.

Unit Focus

Inquiry studies: self-selected topics of research and sharing

Content Objectives

☐ I can research a topic of interest.
☐ I can use nonfiction text features to represent my understanding.
☐ I can locate and cite relevant sources.

Language Objectives

☐ I can ask questions about a topic of interest.
☐ I can read informational books to find information about my topic.
☐ I can write my understandings in my own words.

Cornerstone Text

Will vary depending on topic of research

Anchor Lesson Teaching Procedures

Day 1

1. Explain that students are going to research a topic of their choice and share their research with peers, teachers, and family members.
2. Have students choral read the objectives aloud with you.
3. Give students an example of something you are interested in researching. Ask students to turn and talk in pairs about something they would be interested in researching. Have each student write down five ideas.

4. If possible, go to the library and/or computer lab to explore resources on their top three ideas. This exploratory time should help them narrow the topic down to one. Ask students to submit their topic to you.

Day 2

1. Prior to meeting with students, work with the librarian to collect as many books and resources as possible on their topics.
2. Have students choral read the objectives aloud with you.
3. Show students examples of previous research posters and reports. (See examples in Chapters Three and Seven.)
4. Remind them of tools they have used for previous research: reading, taking notes, asking questions, documenting their thinking, documenting what they learned, summarizing information, making connections, quoting important information, citing sources, representing information in meaningful ways (using nonfiction text features), and discussing their thinking with peers.
5. Review the list of nonfiction text features students have identified in previous lessons with visual examples (place sticky notes labeling these in sample books for a brief review and reference tool): table of contents, index, illustrations, photographs, labels, captions, models, diagrams, cutaways, charts, maps, key terms, headings, summaries, citations, bibliographies, annotated bibliographies, glossary, and so on.
6. Explain that their menu of options for independent inquiry on their topic is listed on the researcher chart. They can be doing any of those things during independent inquiry (see sample inquiry menu/checklist in Chapter Three).
7. Have students turn and talk about their goal for the independent inquiry time period. Ask them to write this down with the date in an inquiry notebook or folder. Tell them you will be checking on their progress at the end of the period.
8. Show students the resources and have them get started. For topics that your school library or even public library does not have resources, you can have students choose one of their other topics or you can have them do their research online. Your librarian can help you identify online resources and databases to which your district subscribes that have appropriate content for your students.
9. Bring students back together and ask them to talk with a partner about how well they accomplished their goal. Both students give a rating on each other's papers from 1 to 4: 1 = I didn't come close to meeting my goal; 2 = I partially met my goal; 3 = I completely met my goal; 4 = I met my goal and made additional progress.

10. Revisit content and language objectives. Ask students to turn and talk about which, if any, objectives they met during this first independent inquiry session.

Stories from the Classroom

I was working with a fifth-grade teacher in a transitional language classroom where the majority of instruction was presented in English, but the bilingual teacher supported English learners in Spanish (language, materials, writing, etc.) as needed. We were beginning their end-of-the year research unit, and I was helping teach the anchor lessons and small groups and support independent inquiry for six weeks. I placed my Pilates instructor training materials, online article printouts, and books on the history, practice, and modification of Pilates on the front whiteboard railing. I told the fifth-grade class we were going to be researching a topic of interest, and I explained I was interested in Pilates because I was studying and training for my certification program. I told them they were going to have the opportunity to research a topic of interest to them, and I explained it could be researching anything of interest (that was appropriate) such as animals, habitats, science concepts, a historic event, famous people, and so on. I explained this research would serve as their final fifth-grade research project (all fifth graders in this school were required to write a research report and present it at the end of the year). We choral read the objectives aloud, and I told students they would be working on their independent inquiry during workshop time during the upcoming six weeks.

I asked students to brainstorm ideas for topics with a partner and write down five ideas. We went to the library to look for resources on their top three topic selections. The librarian helped half the class search for books on students' topics, while I took the other half of the class to the computer lab to search online. Although everyone found at least something online, the library did not have books on all of the topics. For example, we couldn't find any books on Heber's topic of choice, Mexican cowboys, *caballeros*. I told students to consider all the resources they examined, pick their topic for their inquiry project, and write it down on a piece of paper. We had a couple of new students at the Starting stage who wrote it in Spanish and then translated it.

That night I went to the public library and collected any additional resources I could find. The next day I asked students to choral read the objectives for workshop time with me again. I showed them examples of second-grade research posters and projects (I didn't have any models from older grades at that time) and explained that we would be doing more elaborate and sophisticated versions of these posters. I reminded students that we already knew a lot about research and nonfiction text. I referred to the What We Do When We Are Researching chart and asked students to read it aloud with me. Then, we did the same with the chart of nonfiction text features. I told them they could use any of the options from the researching anchor chart, but they needed to set goals for their independent workshop time. They shared with a partner and started working.

One of the new Starting English learners wanted to research an animal from Mexico, so he spent time reading and taking notes. He was determined to write in English, so he frequently referred to his translation dictionary. On the first workshop day, he managed to write a question about what Mexican spotted owls look like, sketch an image, write information about the length of their wingspan, and document a new vocabulary word (*incubate*). This first day we did not pull small groups, but instead walked around and supported the English learners as they needed help and made suggestions for differentiated independent inquiry. I called the students together and they were excited as they evaluated themselves and their partner on the day's progress. As we choral read the objectives and I asked if they thought they accomplished them, Julio said, "I did some, but it's gonna take a lot of time before we get all of them." I agreed and explained this was part of the inquiry process we would be working on over the six weeks.

Following are some ideas for differentiation, teacher roles, and student expectations that we used to modify instructional support for these students.

Differentiation and Considerations According to Proficiency Levels

Stages of Language Proficiency	Teacher Roles	English Learner Expectations/Performance
STAGE 1: *Preproduction Silent Period (Starting)*	☐ Use slowed speech and emphasize nonfiction text features chart. ☐ Point out and provide additional realia and images to support students' comprehension of the selected inquiry topic. ☐ Read aloud or have a peer read aloud to students. ☐ When possible, pair the student with a classmate who speaks the student's first language. ☐ Allow students to read and write in their first language, when possible. ☐ Encourage translation, when possible. ☐ When conferring with stage 1 students, focus on image with the possibility of labels and captions.	☐ Will mostly likely be unable to choral read the objectives. ☐ Can listen to teacher or partner read aloud. ☐ Can copy or create images. ☐ Can use first language to document learning. ☐ Can use Spanish–English translation dictionary. ☐ May be able to copy image and brief label.

(continues)

Stages of Language Proficiency (continued)	Teacher Roles	English Learner Expectations/Performance
STAGE 2: *Early Production (Emerging)*	☐ Use slowed speech and emphasize nonfiction text features chart. ☐ Point out and provide additional realia and images to support students' comprehension of the selected inquiry topic. ☐ Read aloud or have a peer read aloud to students. ☐ When possible, pair with a classmate who speaks the student's first language. ☐ Allow students to read and write in their first language, when possible. ☐ Encourage translation, when necessary. ☐ Provide sentence starters for captions. Example: This is a picture of _____. ☐ When conferring with stage 2 students, focus on images, labels, and captions. Scribe captions when possible and encourage discussion and sharing with peers.	☐ Might be able to choral read parts of the objectives. ☐ Can use first language to document learning. ☐ Can use Spanish-English translation dictionary. ☐ Can create images with simple labels. ☐ Can attempt to fill in the blank and copy the sentence starter. ☐ Can share simple labels or a brief copied or scribed caption in partners or small groups after having a chance to practice/rehearse.
STAGE 3: *Speech Emergence (Developing)*	☐ Have students participate in a paired reading and discussion about nonfiction text features and their topic of inquiry. ☐ Encourage students to create questions, image, label, caption, basic summary, bibliography, and glossary (in English). ☐ Encourage students to share different inquiry research options and findings with peers (image, label, caption, basic summary, bibliography, and glossary).	☐ Can choral read objectives. ☐ Can participate in partner and independent reading of nonfiction text (appropriate level). ☐ Can ask questions, find information, and document learning with images, labels captions, basic summaries, bibliographies, glossaries. ☐ Can share documentation of learning with small or whole group after having a chance to practice/rehearse.
STAGE 4: *Intermediate Fluency (Expanding)*	☐ Have students participate in paired or independent reading. ☐ Have students create questions, images, labels, captions, summaries, a bibliography, and a glossary in their own words. ☐ Encourage students to document their learning using additional nonfiction text features. ☐ Encourage students to discuss and share with partners, small group, and whole class.	☐ Can choral read objectives. ☐ Can participate in independent or paired reading of grade-level nonfiction texts. ☐ Can ask questions and find answers in multiple nonfiction sources. ☐ Can document learning utilizing nonfiction text features including, but not limited to: images, labels, captions, bold words, headings, diagrams, tables, cutaways, maps, glossary, bibliography, summary. ☐ Can share research, writing, and thinking with classmates.

Stages of Language Proficiency (continued)	Teacher Roles	English Learner Expectations/Performance
STAGE 5: *Advanced Fluency (Bridging)*	☐ Encourage students to move beyond initial instruction and modeling by providing the written information in their own words, identifying difficult vocabulary with accompanying explanations. ☐ Encourage discussion of why research on this topic is important, and ask students to make connections to other students' research.	☐ Can choral read objectives. ☐ Can ask questions and find answers in multiple nonfiction sources. ☐ Can document new learning with a wide variety of nonfiction text features. ☐ Can identify and define difficult vocabulary. ☐ Can discuss reasoning for why this research is important and make connections to other students' research.

This type of independent inquiry can be done in any grade level with modifications. Figures 5.4 and 5.5 are images of Rachel Busetti Frevert's second-grade bilinguals all working at different stages of their independent inquiry. In Figure 5.4 you can see the class full of English learners working on their research at various stages during workshop time. Figure 5.5 is a picture of an English learner working on his independent inquiry during workshop time.

Figure 5.4
Workshop Time

Figure 5.5
Independent Work

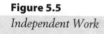

Figure 5.5
Independent Work

Children's Literature Suggestions (Primary)

Berger, Melvin, and Gilda Berger. 2000. *Do Tarantulas Have Teeth? Questions and Answers About Poisonous Creatures*. New York: Scholastic.

Carney, Elizabeth. 2009. *National Geographic Readers: Mummies*. Washington, D.C.: National Geographic Kids.

Delano, Marfe Fergason. 2014. *Explore My World: Butterflies*. Washington, D.C.: National Geographic Kids.

Floca, Brian. 2014. *Locomotive*. New York: Atheneum Books for Young Readers.

Zoefeld, Kathy. 2011. *National Geographic Readers: Trains*. Washington, D.C.: National Geographic Kids.

Children's Literature Suggestions (Intermediate)

Aguilar, David. 2013. *Space Encyclopedia*. Washington, D.C.: National Geographic Kids.

Kindersley, Dorling. 2005. *Vietnam War*. New York: DK Publishing.

King, David C. 2008. *First People*. New York: DK Publishing.

Platt, Richard. 2001. *Extreme Sports*. New York: DK Publishing.

Stone, Tonya Lee. 2014. *Courage Has No Color: The True Story of the Triple Nickles, America's First Black Paratroopers*. Somerville, MA: Candlewick Press.

Assessment

The same questions about assessment during guided learning experiences during workshop time that apply with informational text also apply with fiction texts. Although the answer to the first question ("Were the students on task and did they use their time for academic purposes?") is the same, the responses to the second two questions are slightly different.

QUESTION 2: How were the students using and applying their knowledge? Did we meet the objectives?

The objectives with independent inquiry will never be accomplished in one lesson or one day. These are long-term objectives that students might partially meet day to day. But, even when they have met a single objective, they continue with the process because it is the culmination of the objectives being met multiple times that leads to the final inquiry project and presentation. Observing students participating in independent inquiry during guided learning experiences during workshop time before you actually start working with small groups or conferring will give you a great deal of insight about how the English learners are applying their language, literacy, and research strategies. As English learners are working, you can provide suggestions and feedback to support their independence (see suggestions for differentiation in the previous chart). This might include text or resource suggestions, language frames for documenting learning, vocabulary support, or reading aloud and discussing.

When observing, keep a list of ways students are applying their knowledge. A simple rubric or checklist that includes the items from the research and nonfiction text features chart can be a great way to keep track of how each student is developing in the research process. Additionally, keep anecdotal notes on ways English learners are using language and areas of language development that might need more focus (academic language, syntax, etc.).

QUESTION 3: Where do they need additional instruction and support?

Based on your observations and analysis of their inquiry notebook or folder, you will be able to see areas of need. This was how I created my small groups. For example, I noticed some students were only using the labels, captions, images, and "I learned" language frame to document their new learning, so I had a small-group session with those students, reviewing additional strategies for research and documenting their learning. We reviewed note-taking, summaries, and glossaries, and then I asked them to apply one of those to their research. In the small group, I could provide immediate feedback as they applied the concepts to their own work—again, providing another opportunity for me to assess how they were using and applying their skills while simultaneously supporting what they would be able to do without me during this time the following day.

There was a group of four Starting English learners who needed assistance understanding difficult sections of their books and additional language support to write and convey what they were learning. I pulled this group of students to help with reading parts of text on demand as well as suggesting and reviewing language frames to help them document their thinking: I wonder _____; I think _____; I learned _____; This is a picture of _____. These language frames allowed students to begin communicating what they were learning. These informal observations and inquiry folder assessments followed by conferring and small-group differentiation helped guide my thinking about the next minilesson, differentiation, and scaffolding.

Reflection

☐ What are some ways you could expand on opportunities for choice during English learners' independent/guided learning experiences time?

☐ What are your current options for independent work or reading while you are meeting with small groups and conferring? Are there ways you could make that time more meaningful?

☐ How might you support language and literacy development during guided learning experiences? How will you differentiate?

☐ How will you plan, document, and assess English learners' work during guided learning experiences?

☐ What guided learning experiences will you add to your menu of options for your upcoming units of study?

CHAPTER 6

Small-Group Instruction and Word Work

"THERE IS SUCH A HUGE VARIETY OF ABILITY AND LANGUAGE LEVELS IN MY classroom. Some kids are reading novels and others don't know their letters and sounds. I have a new student from Mongolia, and she doesn't speak a word of English. It feels impossible to reach everyone, but the expectation is that students will all be reading 'complex texts' [she made quotation marks with her fingers]. How is that possible?" A veteran second-grade teacher voiced her frustrations at the start of our professional development day together. I agreed with her—teachers are faced with the immense responsibility of reaching and providing appropriate instruction for all of their students, and sometimes that task feels impossible. Although there are options for differentiating whole-group instruction, small-group instruction is an opportunity to provide targeted instruction based on English learners' needs and interests in multilingual classroom settings.

■ Broad Overview: What is it? Why do we do it? How do we plan for it?

Small-group time should support English learners in a variety of ways including, but not limited to, guided reading, strategy instruction, vocabulary instruction, sheltering/front-loading/reviewing, supported literature circles, fluency, and word work or decoding skills. This time provides the scaffolding necessary to better support participation in whole-class work as well as foster independence during the guided learning experiences. All small-group instruction should connect back to students' independent reading practice. Even when teaching phonics and decoding strategies, these skills should always have a connection to text and English learners' independent reading and responding after they leave the small group.

The tendency is to group students according to scores on literacy assessments or English language proficiency. I would caution against these types of long-term grouping techniques. Experts in the field suggest flexible grouping strategies based on a variety of factors including independent reading level, interest, strategy instruction needs, and random or heterogeneous grouping with frequent opportunities for new groups (Opitz and Ford 2001; Serravallo 2010). I recommend making language an additional consideration for grouping students. English learners can benefit from opportunities working with bilingual peers while the teacher provides additional language support and sheltering (Echevarria, Short, and Vogt 2008) to scaffold an upcoming whole-group lesson or review and reinforce one that was just taught (August et al. 2005). In addition to working with other bilinguals, English learners also need time to work in small groups with highly proficient English speakers. This is why flexible grouping is a must for classrooms with English learners.

For elementary classrooms, focus your planning and small-group time for English learners in the following ways: front-loading or reviewing/reinforcing whole-group lessons; guided reading and fluency; literature circles; comprehension strategy instruction; and word work and decoding. Front-loading whole-group lessons can be used when the teacher anticipates the English learner will need extra support to participate in a lesson. A focus on vocabulary, context, exposure, and language support is used to prepare students for a whole-group lesson. Likewise, teachers review and reinforce language and content concepts following whole-group instruction for English learners who need the additional support.

Guided reading and fluency-focused groups are typically "ability" grouped according to the students' instructional text level. The texts are selected by the teacher, and the small-group instruction usually begins with a book introduction followed by reading with coaching. The session finishes with teacher suggestions and/or discussion. I highly encourage at least some discussion about comprehension because the read-aloud fluency of English learners can be deceiving, particularly if they learned to decode in their first language. English learners may be reading aloud with ease, but they might need additional support with vocabulary and comprehension.

Literature circles have been shown to strengthen literacy skills and confidence of English learners (Carrison and Ernst-Slavit 2005). Teachers of English learners select books with rich language, multicultural themes, interesting plots, and strong characters and give a brief book talk (oral preview). English learners then review books and select their top two choices. Students are grouped according to preferences (not ability) and plan reading goals on a group calendar. Students then meet in their groups to read and discuss their books. I recommend giving English learners the opportunity to read with a buddy or with a taped recording of the book when needed. Students write reading responses to prepare for discussions and complete a culminating project to demonstrate their understanding of the book to share with peers (see my suggestions for English learner support and differentiation for this in Chapter Five). Sometimes it's necessary for the teacher to help guide and facilitate the literature discussion groups during the first couple sessions, but then literature circles can become part of guided learning experiences during the workshop time.

Comprehension strategy instruction with English learners is similar to what is advocated with English speakers (Harvey and Goudvis 2000) because all readers build on their background knowledge to construct meaning with text. However, English learners are often drawing on very different cultural and linguistic backgrounds than those of the students for which the curriculum was originally designed (Herrera, Perez, and Escamilla 2010). Because of this, teachers must consider English learners' sociocultural, linguistic, and academic knowledge to select appropriate texts and strategy instruction.

Word recognition, vocabulary, and decoding skills also play a vital role in the fluency and comprehension development of English learners (Herrera, Perez, and Escamilla 2010; Helman et al. 2011). However, not all students need support with phonics and decoding skills. Word work (which includes phonics, spelling, and vocabulary) should be done in needs-based small groups. Explicit instruction, modeling, and guided practice can facilitate the development of these skills, but it is crucial to ground these skills in the context of reading actual books. Students must be able to do more than decode or encode words; they need to understand the meaning and see the word in context. Simply having the English learners complete spelling activities and words sorts can be a waste of time if they do not yet possess the vocabulary to comprehend the words out of context. The application and purpose of developing these skills should always be to support their reading of real texts.

Specific Ideas for Instruction (Fiction and Informational Focus)

In the following sections, I include sample small-group lessons including the content and language objectives, cornerstone text, teaching procedures, vignettes from the classrooms, and samples of student work and interactions. I provide suggestions for differentiation according to stages of language proficiency, children's literature suggestions, and ways to assess students. There are endless options for small-group instruction and word work, but the key is that it should target the needs of your English learners. In this chapter, I share a primary word work and decoding lesson using a scavenger hunt and interactive poetry writing, a primary lesson with an informational text and summarizing focus, and an intermediate lesson with a fictional text focus.

Primary Word Work and Decoding: Word Family Scavenger Hunt and Poetry Creation

Content Objectives
- ☐ I can identify words in the -*at* family.
- ☐ I can help create an -*at* family poem.

Language Objectives
- ☐ I can read -*at* family words.
- ☐ I can read our -*at* family poem out loud.

Cornerstone Text
The Cat in the Hat (Seuss 1957)

Anchor Lesson Teaching Procedures

1. Select a quality text with multiple examples of the word work or decoding concept you would like to teach.
2. Utilize a document camera or have copies of the book for students to read along during the read-aloud. Also prepare a chart that says, "If I can spell *at*, I can also spell . . ." (could be any word family).
3. Choral read (or read aloud) the content and language objectives.
4. Tell students they are going to go on an -*at* family word hunt, so they will be looking and listening for words in the story that end with *at*. Read the title aloud as an example and identify the two words (*cat* and *hat*).

5. Read aloud, drawing attention to words in the -*at* family. Ask students to put a finger on the -*at* family word and another finger in the air when you read an -*at* family word.

6. After the read-aloud scavenger hunt, draw students' attention to the chart and explain that if they can spell *at*, they can also spell *cat* and *hat*. Ask students to turn and talk to come up with three other -*at* family words. They can be from the book or just words they know rhyme.

7. Add the words to the chart with a small sketch beside them (to support vocabulary).

8. Explain that students are going to use these words to create an -*at* family poem, and model the first line asking a student to come and finish the -*at* family word. For example, if you say, "There was a boy named Pat." Write "There was a boy named P__" and ask a student to write *at* to finish.

9. Ask students to turn and talk and come up with another line. Scribe their sentence, but leave the entire -*at* family word blank for them to write. Add pictures to support wherever possible.

10. Complete the poem and choral read as a small group. Ask the students to stand up every time they read an -*at* word. Tell them that they will be revisiting this poem over the next couple of days and that they will have an opportunity to create their own poem.

11. Revisit the content and language objectives.

Stories from the Classroom

In a kindergarten classroom of eighteen students with seven English learners, many students were still working on learning letters and sounds. Based on observations, I created a needs-based group. The students in the group all needed additional support for decoding and encoding CVC (consonant–vowel–consonant) words, and five of the six students were English learners (at varying language proficiency levels). I had copies of *The Cat in the Hat* (Seuss 1957) for all six students in the small group. I read the objectives aloud to the students and explained that we were going to be "word hunters" today. We were looking for any words that were members of the -*at* family during our read-aloud. I pointed to the words as I read the title aloud and asked students to turn and talk with a partner about any -*at* words they noticed. Maria and Sarai shouted out, "*Cat* and *hat*!" before some of the other students even had a chance to talk. I explained I would be reading the book aloud while they followed along with their fingers, and we would play Finger On, Finger Up with -*at* family words. (Finger On, Finger Up was a game we played when we were looking for vocabulary words, word family words, punctuation, etc. It was a relatively quiet way to signal they identified in the text the skill or word we were learning about.)

I began reading aloud, and together we modeled putting a finger on and a finger up when I read the first -*at* word (*sat*). I reread the page and asked students to try it on their own this time. We continued with the read-aloud and Finger On, Finger Up. When I was done reading, I explained we were going to be creating an -*at* word family chart because if they can spell *at*, they can spell anything in the word family. I gave the examples of *cat* and *hat* and added them to the chart, underlining *at* in each word, and I added a quick sketch to represent the word. Then, I asked them to turn and talk with their partner to come up with three more words to add to the chart. We added their words with sketches when appropriate.

Then, I told students we were going to use these words to make our own -*at* family poem. I modeled the first line by saying, "There once was a boy named Pat." I scribed my words on chart paper, but stopped after the *P* and asked students what I needed to do to finish it. They all chimed in, "Add *at*!" I asked Maria if she could add it for me, so she came up and added *at*. I then asked students to turn and talk to come up with the next line that needed to end with an -*at* word. Jules and Tony came up with "He liked to wear a hat." I wrote the first part of the sentence, but asked Jules to write their -*at* word. Together each group had a chance to add at least one line and we came up with the following "At Word Family Poem":

> There once was a boy named Pat
> He liked to wear a hat
> He carried a bat
> He had a cat
> Who ate a rat

We choral read the poem together once. Then, I asked students to choral read it again, but stand up every time they read an -*at* word. They read the poem aloud and giggled as they stood up for -*at* words. I explained we would be reading this poem again tomorrow and the next day, and they were going to have a chance to write poems with partners and then by themselves.

Differentiation and Considerations According to Proficiency Levels

Stages of Language Proficiency	Teacher Roles	English Learner Expectations/Performance
STAGE 1: *Preproduction Silent Period (Starting)*	☐ Use slowed speech and emphasize vocabulary by pointing to, gesturing, and repeating essential words during the read-aloud. ☐ Provide visual cues like underlining *at* on chart. ☐ Allow students to work with a partner for word identification and poem creation. ☐ When possible, pair the student with a classmate who speaks the student's first language.	☐ Will mostly likely be unable to choral read the objectives. ☐ Can point to *-at* words. ☐ Can listen to teacher or partner read aloud. ☐ Might be able to copy *-at* words. ☐ Can attempt to participate in Finger On, Figure Up.
STAGE 2: *Early Production (Emerging)*	☐ Use slowed speech and emphasize vocabulary by pointing to, gesturing, and repeating essential words during the read-aloud. ☐ Provide visual cues like underlining *at* on chart. ☐ Allow students to work with a partner for word identification and poem creation. ☐ When possible, pair the student with a classmate who speaks the student's first language. ☐ Provide sentence starters for *-at* family poem. Examples: He saw a ___ at. He had a ___at. ☐ Invite students to choral read the poem.	☐ Might be able to choral read parts of the objectives. ☐ Can identify *-at* words. ☐ Might be able to identify *-at* words not found in the story. ☐ Can attempt to fill in the blank of the sentence starter to create a line for the *-at* family poem. ☐ Can share language frame/sentence starter response in small group after having a chance to practice/rehearse with a partner. ☐ Might be able to choral read parts of the poem.
STAGE 3: *Speech Emergence (Developing)*	☐ Provide visual cues like underlining *at* on chart. ☐ Have students participate in Finger On, Finger Up. ☐ Allow students to work with a partner for word identification, word creation, and line of the poem creation. ☐ Provide sentence starters for *-at* family poem. Examples: He saw a ___ at. He had a ___at. ☐ Encourage students to share their responses with a partner before coming to the chart to write their *-at* word in the poem. ☐ Ask students to choral read the poem.	☐ Can choral read objectives. ☐ Can identify *-at* words. ☐ Can identify *-at* words not found in the story. ☐ Can fill in the blank of the sentence starter to create a line for the *-at* family poem. ☐ Can share language frame/sentence starter response and write *-at* word on the chart in the small group after having a chance to practice/rehearse with a partner. ☐ Can choral read the poem.

Stages of Language Proficiency *(continued)*	Teacher Roles	English Learner Expectations/Performance
STAGE 4: *Intermediate Fluency (Expanding)*	☐ Have students participate in Finger On, Finger Up. ☐ Allow students to work with a partner for word identification, word creation, and line of the poem creation. ☐ Ask students to create the line of the poem using their own words (moving away from the language frames). ☐ Encourage students to share their responses with a partner before coming to the chart to write their *-at* word in the poem. ☐ Encourage students to create their own *-at* family poem using the *-at* family chart. ☐ Ask students to identify *-at* family words in their independent reading.	☐ Can choral read objectives. ☐ Can identify *-at* words. ☐ Can identify *-at* words not found in the story. ☐ Can create the line of the poem using their own words (moving away from the language frames). ☐ Can share the line of poetry and write *-at* word on the chart in the small group after having a chance to practice/rehearse with a partner. ☐ Can create their own *-at* family poem using the *-at* family chart. ☐ Can identify *-at* family words in their independent reading.
STAGE 5: *Advanced Fluency (Bridging)*	☐ Have students participate in Finger On, Finger Up. ☐ Allow students to work with a partner for word identification, word creation, and line of the poem creation. ☐ Ask students to create the line of the poem using their own words (moving away from the language frames). ☐ Encourage students to share their responses with a partner before coming to the chart to write their *-at* word in the poem. ☐ Encourage students to create their own *-at* family poem and other word family poems. ☐ Encourage self-selected word family scavenger hunts in their independent reading.	☐ Can choral read objectives. ☐ Can identify *-at* words. ☐ Can identify *-at* words not found in the story. ☐ Can create and share the line of poetry and write *-at* word on the chart in the small group after having a chance to practice/rehearse with a partner. ☐ Can create their own *-at* family poem. ☐ Can create additional word family poems. ☐ Can complete self-selected word family scavenger hunts in their independent reading.

There are many different types of instruction that can be used for word work and decoding strategies in small groups and transitioning to independent work. In Figure 6.1, you will notice a first-grade English learner in Rachael Pritchard's class identifying and adding words from her reading into her word work folder categories. This is a perfect example of teaching word work and decoding skills and linking them to independent reading and practice. In the suggested children's literature found below, I only recommend primary books because word family rhyming would not be appropriate in most intermediate classrooms.

Figure 6.1
Word Work

Children's Literature Suggestions (Primary)

Beaton, Claire. 2002. *How Big Is a Pig?* Concord, MA: Barefoot Books.

Beaumont, Karen. 2005. *I Ain't Gonna Paint No More!* New York: HMH Books for Young Readers.

Blackstone, Stella. 2005. *My Granny Went to Market*. Concord, MA: Barefoot Books.

Brown, Margaret Wise. 1995. *Big Red Barn*. New York: Harper Collins.

———. 2005. *Good Night Moon*. New York: Harper Collins.

Dr. Seuss. 1957. *The Cat in the Hat*. New York: Random House.

———. 1963. *Hop on Pop*. New York: Random House.

Elya, Susan Middleton. 2003. *No More, Por Favor*. New York: Putnam Publishing Group.

———. 2003. *Oh No, Gotta Go!* New York: Putnam Publishing Group.

———. 2008. *Tooth on the Loose*. New York: Putnam Publishing Group.

Assessment

Assessment for meeting this lesson's objectives can be easily completed using observation during the small-group session. Additional assessment information I wanted for this particular lesson was to find out if the English learners were able to take the skills we practiced and use them the following day during our repeated reading and, eventually, during their independent reading and writing. Observation of student reading and student writing was the best way to discover this information. As English learners continued to learn more word families, running records were insightful to gaining a better understanding of which word families they were identifying independently. Some teachers create a checklist of decoding skills and/or word families that small groups have worked on to use as an informal assessment to analyze English learners' independent reading. This information then guides future instruction and possible reteaching during small-group time.

It is important to note that when English learners are reading aloud for a running record, dialect or accents that affect pronunciation should not be counted as miscues. Additionally, even when focusing on decoding, it is essential to check for and support comprehension with discussion, visual cues, and vocabulary support. Meaning making and language support are crucial for English learners regardless of what decoding skill is being taught. The purpose of word recognition and decoding skills is to better support their ability to engage with and comprehend text. Nonsense words and meaningless phonics readers can be confusing to students who are trying to learn a new language—they are confusing to me, and English is my first language!

Primary Lesson: Supporting Inquiry with Strategies for Informational Text

This needs-based lesson assumes students have been introduced to informational text features and the basics of inquiry research and projects during whole-group anchor lessons. This is for a group of English learners who were copying directly out of the books instead of putting their new learning in their own words. I pulled this small group of English learners for a needs-based comprehension minilesson on summarizing.

Content Objectives
- ☐ I can learn new information about my inquiry topic.
- ☐ I can put my new learning into my own words (summarize).

Language Objectives
- ☐ I can read new information about my inquiry topic.
- ☐ I can write the new information in my own words.

Cornerstone Text
Each student has a different text depending on their inquiry topic. Select one of their texts to use as a model.

Anchor Lesson Teaching Procedures

1. Select a quality informational text that one of the students is using for their inquiry project.
2. Create a chart for teaching summarizing (e.g., Read part of the text. Stop and think about what you read. Sketch and write what you learned using your own words.). See sample chart in Figure 6.2 from Rachel Busetti Frevert's classroom.
3. Choral read (or read aloud) the content and language objectives.
4. Explain to students they are learning and sharing a lot of important information about their topics, but you noticed some students were writing exactly what the author said. Tell them they are the experts, and you want to hear their thinking and new learning in their own words.
5. Refer students to the chart about summarizing and explain the steps using visuals and examples when possible.
6. Read aloud a paragraph from one of their books and ask them to sketch an image and tell a friend what they learned in their own words.
7. Use student examples to add to the chart as an example of a summary.
8. Ask students to read and then summarize one sentence in their book with a partner.
9. Encourage students to work on summarizing with their own informational text and inquiry projects while you support them during small-group time.

Stories from the Classroom

The bilingual second graders (all students in the class were learning English as their second language) were doing an inquiry-based unit on natural disasters in English. During whole-group lessons, I modeled reading information and writing captions or paragraphs in my own words, and many students were doing the same. However, I noticed a small group of students who were copying the images and captions directly from the books. When asked to read their writing and talk about what they learned, they did not know what many of the vocabulary words meant. I asked that group of students to join me at the back table during small-group instruction. I explained that we were going to be practicing putting ideas into our own words because we were the authors and experts of our work. I reminded them that we would still have our citation list where we got our information (we would photocopy the cover or title of the book and author and glue it onto their poster), but we needed to put our new learning into our own words.

We choral read the content and language objectives together before I showed them a chart with the following information and visuals about summarizing:

1. Read the sentence, paragraph, or page. (This had a sketch of a stick figure reading.)
2. Stop (sketch of a stop sign) and think about what you learned (sketch of stick figure with a lightbulb and finger to the temple area).
3. Sketch the big idea (sketch of paper with sketch on it).
4. Write what you learned in your own words (sketch of writing).

Then, I asked Angel to borrow his book on earthquakes. I read a page aloud and asked the English learners to do a quick sketch of what they learned. They then shared their sketch and told a partner what they learned in their own words. I asked for student volunteers and wrote their example under step 4 on the summarizing chart. I asked students to use their own books to try one and share with a partner. The English learners all completed a brief sketch and summary and shared with a partner. I instructed them to continue to use the summarizing strategy while I worked with individual students. See Figure 4.4 for a sample student summary of a storm surge. It's important to note that a summarizing lesson is not appropriate for all levels of language proficiency, especially in a needs-based small group. You will notice I omitted teacher roles and English learner expectations for the first two stages of language proficiency for the differentiation considerations related to this lesson.

Differentiation and Considerations According to Proficiency Levels

Stages of Language Proficiency	Teacher Roles	English Learner Expectations/Performance
STAGE 1: *Preproduction Silent Period (Starting)*	☐ I would not recommend teaching summarizing to English learners in this stage.	
STAGE 2: *Early Production (Emerging)*	☐ I would not recommend teaching summarizing to English learners in this stage.	
STAGE 3: *Speech Emergence (Developing)*	☐ Have students participate in a paired reading and discussion about summary. ☐ Ask students to sketch, write, and share a basic summary. ☐ Encourage students to share summary with a partner before sharing with the small group.	☐ Can choral read objectives. ☐ Can participate in a partner reading of nonfiction text (appropriate level). ☐ Might be able to sketch, write, and share a very basic summary. ☐ Can share sketch and writing with small group after having a chance to practice/rehearse.

(continues)

Stages of Language Proficiency (continued)	Teacher Roles	English Learner Expectations/Performance
STAGE 4: *Intermediate Fluency (Expanding)*	☐ Have students participate in a paired reading and discussion about summary. ☐ Ask students to sketch, write, and share a summary using and explaining a new academic vocabulary term. ☐ Encourage students to share summary with a partner before sharing with the small group.	☐ Can choral read objectives. ☐ Can participate in a partner reading of grade-level, nonfiction text. ☐ Can sketch, write, and share a summary. ☐ Can use and explain new academic vocabulary. ☐ Can share sketch and writing with small group after having a chance to practice/rehearse.
STAGE 5: *Advanced Fluency (Bridging)*	☐ Have students participate in a paired reading and discussion about summary. ☐ Ask students to sketch, write, and share a summary using and explaining two to three new academic vocabulary terms. ☐ Encourage students to summarize across texts and topic areas: for example, summarizing ideas from multiple sources and making connections among other natural disasters and/or science concepts.	☐ Can choral read objectives. ☐ Can identify examples and purpose of image labels and captions. ☐ Can document new learning with self-created image, labels, captions, and summaries. ☐ Can identify and define difficult vocabulary. ☐ Can summarize across texts and topic areas by making connections to other natural disasters and science concepts.

Small-group lessons supporting comprehension of informational text and inquiry should be adapted to fit the needs of your English learners. For example, Figure 6.2 includes an anchor chart from a small-group lesson focused on summarizing and synthesizing with second-grade bilinguals in Rachel Busetti Frevert's class.

Children's Literature Suggestions (Primary)

Rattini, Kristin Baird. 2013. *National Geographic Readers: Weather*. Washington, D.C.: National Geographic Kids.

Simon, Seymour. 1988. *Volcanoes*. New York: Harper Collins.

———. 2001. *Tornadoes*. New York: Harper Collins.

———. 2006. *Weather*. New York: Harper Collins.

———. 2007. *Hurricanes*. New York: Harper Collins.

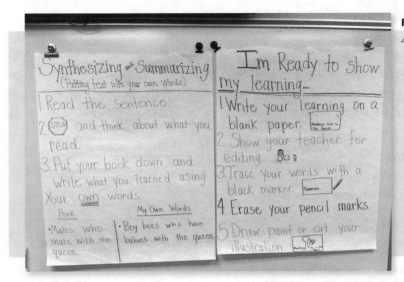

Figure 6.2
Anchor Chart

Children's Literature Suggestions (Intermediate)

Carney, Elizabeth. 2012. *Everything Weather*. Washington, D.C.: National Geographic Kids.

Cosgrove, Brian. 2007. *Eyewitness Books: Weather*. New York: DK Publishers.

Fradin, Judy, and Denis. 2007. *Witness to Disaster: Hurricanes*. Washington, D.C.: National Geographic Kids.

Griffey, Harriet. 2010. *Earthquakes and Other Natural Disasters*. New York: DK Publishing.

Rose, Susan Van. 2008. *Volcanoes and Earthquakes*. New York: DK Publishers.

Assessment

Assessment for meeting this lesson's objectives can best be accomplished using observation during the small-group session and analysis of English learners' writing and research. Additional observational assessment data collected over the following days and weeks helped me document whether the English learners were able to take the summarizing skills we practiced and use them during their independent reading and writing about their topic of inquiry. Observations of this provided important information about students who needed reteaching, additional scaffolding during small group, and/or one-on-one conferring.

Intermediate Lesson: Word Work—Idioms

Adapted from the "What Does It Mean?" lesson in *Comprehension and English Language Learners*
(Opitz and Guccione 2009).

This lesson focuses on idioms, but with a word work unit or extended focus, I suggest slight adaptations and include a range of categories of figurative language such as imagery, simile, metaphor, alliteration, personification, onomatopoeia, and hyperbole.

Content Objectives

☐ I can identify idioms.

☐ I can create an idiom dictionary.

Language Objective

☐ I can read idioms and draw a picture of their literal and intended meanings.

Cornerstone Text

Thank You, Amelia Bedelia (Parish 1995)

Anchor Lesson Teaching Procedures

1. Select a book that contains idioms (or other figurative language focus).
2. Choral read the content and language objectives.
3. Read the text aloud, and stop after the first idiom.
4. Ask students to turn and talk about the literal and intended meaning for the idiom.
5. Have a volunteer share their thoughts while you model their first idiom dictionary entry on chart paper. This dictionary could be in a spiral notebook or separate pages stapled together. It should include three columns: idiom, literal meaning, and intended meaning.
6. In the literal meaning and intended meaning columns, include a sketch to accompany the text. (See example below from Opitz and Guccione [2009] in Figure 6.3.)
7. Tell students that you will be using this dictionary to identify idioms, their literal meaning, and their intended meaning with accompanying illustrations.
8. Give students time to copy their first entry into their idiom dictionary.
9. Provide guided practice as you continue reading *Thank You, Amelia Bedelia* together until you feel students can work in partners without your guidance.
10. Explain that they will continue to add new entries to their idiom dictionary as they encounter them when reading independently or when talking with others.

Idiom	Literal Meaning	Intended Meaning
Raining cats and dogs	Cats and dogs are falling out of clouds in the sky.	Raining heavily

Figure 6.3 *Sample Idiom Dictionary Entry*

Stories from the Classroom

I was working with an exemplary fourth-grade teacher on effective instructional strategies to support the English learners in her classroom. There were only seven English learners (all in the Expanding or Bridging stages) in her class of twenty-seven students, but she wanted ideas for providing targeted support for these learners. When observing partner reading and conferring in her classroom, I noticed many English learners were quickly reading Amelia Bedelia books. However, they were not laughing or talking about how silly the things she was doing were. When I asked them to talk to me about the story, they retold the literal account of what she did with no mention that she was following the literal meanings and not the intended meanings of things like "draw the drapes" and "pitch the tent." I realized we needed to create a small group to focus on idioms for the English learners who had not been exposed to the intended meanings of idioms. All of the English learners in this group were in the Expanding or Bridging stage of language proficiency.

I had multiple copies of *Thank You, Amelia Bedelia* (Parish 1995), so every student could have a copy. We choral read the content and language objectives aloud, and I explained that idioms do not mean what they sound like. I used the idiom about raining cats and dogs, and showed them my sketch in the literal meaning category. I asked them if that was what it meant. They laughed and said, "No!" I asked them to help me fill out the last column of the idiom dictionary entry to help me explain what the intended meaning was. Luka said, "Raining really bad." I rephrased and wrote "Raining really hard" and sketched a picture. I gave them paper stapled in a book with blank idiom dictionary templates, and I asked them to add this same idiom as their first entry.

I explained we would find many idioms when reading Amelia Bedelia books, so I wanted them to be on the lookout for things she was doing that did not make sense, but aligned with a literal meaning of the text. The students immediately identified that Amelia should not be "stripping" or tearing the sheets, but Luka said, "I don't get it, Miss. Why would she tell her to do that?" I reminded them that sometimes people use idioms like "raining cats and dogs" or "stripping the sheets" to mean something different. I suggested they start by adding the idiom and literal meaning because all of the students understood that part. Then, I asked students to go back, reread, and turn and talk about what they thought the intended meaning was. After rereading and discussion, they agreed the intended meaning was to take the sheets off so she could put clean ones on. Students continued reading with partners and adding idioms to their idiom dictionary. At the end of the reading, we reviewed their entries as a small group, and I encouraged students to continue adding to the dictionary as they found more idioms in their independent reading. See the following chart for some differentiation ideas for this lesson. Like the previous lesson, I would not recommend this type of instruction for students in the Starting or Emerging stages.

Differentiation and Considerations According to Proficiency Levels

Stages of Language Proficiency	Teacher Roles	English Learner Expectations/Performance
STAGE 1: *Preproduction Silent Period (Starting)*	☐ I would not recommend teaching idioms to English learners in this stage.	
STAGE 2: *Early Production (Emerging)*	☐ I would not recommend teaching idioms to English learners in this stage.	
STAGE 3: *Speech Emergence (Developing)*	☐ Have students participate in a paired reading and idiom identification. ☐ Ask students to complete idiom dictionary entries with a partner using a preselected text with multiple opportunities for common examples (Amelia Bedelia or similar texts).	☐ Can participate in partner reading and idiom identification. ☐ Might be able to complete idiom dictionary entries with a partner with preselected text with multiple opportunities for common examples (Amelia Bedelia or similar texts).

Stages of Language Proficiency *(continued)*	Teacher Roles	English Learner Expectations/Performance
STAGE 4: *Intermediate Fluency (Expanding)*	☐ Have students participate in a paired reading and idiom identification. ☐ Ask students to complete idiom dictionary entries with a partner using preselected text with multiple opportunities for common examples (Amelia Bedelia or similar texts). ☐ Encourage students to identify idioms in additional texts they are independently reading and add to their idiom dictionary.	☐ Can participate in partner reading and idiom identification. ☐ Can complete idiom dictionary entries with a partner with preselected text with multiple opportunities for common examples (Amelia Bedelia or similar texts). ☐ Might be able to identify idioms in additional texts they are independently reading and add to their idiom dictionary.
STAGE 5: *Advanced Fluency (Bridging)*	☐ Have students participate in a paired reading and idiom identification. ☐ Ask students to complete idiom dictionary entries with a partner. ☐ Encourage students to identify idioms in additional texts they are independently reading and add to their idiom dictionary. ☐ Introduce additional figurative language considerations and encourage additions to a "figurative language" dictionary.	☐ Can participate in partner reading and idiom identification. ☐ Can complete idiom dictionary entries with a partner. ☐ Can identify idioms in additional texts they are independently reading and add to their idiom dictionary. ☐ Can identify additional figurative language.

Children's Literature Suggestions (Primary)

Parish, Herman. 2011. *Amelia Bedelia Makes a Friend.* New York: Greenwillow Books.

Parish, Peggy. 1992. *Amelia Bedelia.* St. Louis, MO: Turtleback Publishing.

———. 1993. *Thank You, Amelia Bedelia.* New York: Harper Collins.

———. 1994. *Amelia Bedelia and the Surprise Shower.* New York: Harper Collins.

———. 1995. *Play Ball, Amelia Bedelia.* New York: Harper Collins.

Children's Literature Suggestions (Intermediate)

Parish, Herman. 2013. *Amelia Bedelia Chapter Book #1: Amelia Bedelia Means Business.* New York: Greenwillow Books.

———. 2013. *Amelia Bedelia Chapter Book #2: Amelia Bedelia Unleashed.* New York: Greenwillow Books.

———. 2013. *Amelia Bedelia Chapter Book #3: Amelia Bedelia Road Trip.* New York: Greenwillow Books.

———. 2014. *Amelia Bedelia Chapter Book #4: Amelia Bedelia Goes Wild!* New York: Greenwillow Books.

———. 2014. *Amelia Bedelia Chapter Book #5: Amelia Bedelia Shapes Up.* New York: Greenwillow Books.

Assessment

To assess this specific lesson, I utilized observation during the small-group session as English learners read with partners and added to their idiom dictionary. Additionally, I observed students during independent reading time to see if they were adding to their idiom dictionary throughout the week. This type of observation during and following needs-based small-group instruction can provide information about who might need reteaching, additional scaffolding during small group, and/or one-on-one conferring.

Reflection

☐ Consider your current small-group instruction. What type of small-group instruction are you conducting? What specific needs are being addressed during this time? How are you grouping students? What opportunities are you giving English learners for targeted language and literacy support?

☐ In what ways could you enhance your small-group instruction to better support English learners' independent reading?

☐ How will you differentiate your small-group instruction to address second language development and literacy skills?

☐ How will you schedule your small-group time? Create a schedule and specify how students will be grouped, when you will be conferring, and the type of small-group instruction that will be provided.

☐ How will you organize your planning, documentation, and assessment of small-group instruction for your English learners?

CHAPTER 7

Reflection and Sharing

URING MY FIRST YEAR OF TEACHING IN AN ENGLISH INSTRUCTION CLASSROOM
in a bilingual school, I always had the best intentions of revisiting the
objectives, giving my students time to reflect on their work, and checking in with their progress and plans for continued work and development. But we
always seemed to run out of time as I found myself scurrying to get my students to
stop what they were doing, quickly put things away and rush off to recess, specials,
or lunch. To be honest, I am not sure I revisited objectives more than once every
couple of weeks my first year. As I reflected on the past year and set goals for supporting my English learners for the next year, I committed to giving myself and my
students time to reflect on our learning at the end of our reading workshop period,
even if it meant cutting something else a few minutes short. In addition to creating
space for daily reflection and sharing of student progress, I also wanted to devote
more time to meaningful sharing and reflection of culminating projects at the end
of each unit of study.

I had to remind myself that it was not about barreling through the list of guided
learning experiences and reaching a culminating event as fast as possible (or at the
speed I originally anticipated), but it was about meaningful experiences that deepened my English learners' experiences with language and literacy in both academic
and social contexts. To do this, I needed time for reflection and sharing every day and
extended time at the end of the unit for the culminating event and reflection.

Broad Overview: What is it? Why do we do it? How do we plan for it?

Many teachers I work with ask the questions, "Reflection and sharing, what exactly does that entail? And how long will it take?" I always tell them it varies according to grade level, language proficiency levels, unit of study, and culminating projects. There are so many things to consider when thinking about how best to reflect and share about English learners' learning and progress. It is important to consider reading as content (just as you would with your monolingual English speakers) with an additional consideration of second language acquisition. It's easiest to consider this component of the workshop for English learners in two separate categories: daily and culminating. This allows teachers and English learners to check in with daily successes, challenges, questions, and progress while also keeping in mind considerations for the final culminating project that is a representation of their long-term learning throughout the course of the unit of study. Both of these reflections should represent content and language development for English learners in some way.

Daily Reflection and Sharing

One way to think about daily reflection and sharing is what Calkins and Tolan (2010) refer to as "Teaching Share." One of the Teaching Share ideas they recommend is to have students complete reading logs, and they ask children to record, study, and discuss their reading. Typically, the log includes the date, title, and amount of reading (either time or page number). For young children, writing the title and author may take too much time away from reading time because their books are so short that they may read three to four in a twenty-minute period. In this case, students can write the level of book they are reading (assuming the books are leveled) and place a check mark for each book read during the reading period. Calkins and Tolan (2010) recommend having discussions with children and the group about what they notice in their reading life—asking them how things are going, challenges they encounter, successes and integration of new learning. I encourage extending and adapting this to more specifically support your English learners.

In addition to having conversations about reading experiences, including discussions about language acquisition—specifically second language comprehension, strategies, and expressive output—can help English learners reflect on their simultaneous goals and growth in reading and learning English. This might begin with something as simple as using a thumbs up or thumbs down to reflect on how well they met the content and language objectives or having discussions with a peer at the end of the workshop period. As Echevarria, Short, and Vogt (2008) have documented, the introduction and revisiting of content and language objectives are important for effective sheltered instruction for English learners in an English instruction classroom. Then, a discussion as a class about how things are going and how well students felt they met the standards can be used to guide future objectives, set goals, and plan instruction.

Daily reflection can be done independently, but it is beneficial for English learners to have the opportunity to talk with their peers. This allows students to continue to develop their expressive and receptive vocabulary drawing on and expanding their BICS (Basic Interpersonal Communicative Skills) and CALP (Cognitive Academic Language Proficiency) (Cummins 1979). The sharing and expectation of challenges and successes for all students can lower the affective filter (Krashen 1987) and make English learners feel more comfortable and willing to take risks. Adapted reading logs for English learners can be a way to begin with independent reflection followed by discussion with peers (and the entire class when appropriate). Figure 7.1 is an example of a modified reading log for a third-grade English learner. There are two lines for what went well and challenges encountered; they provide entry spaces to identify a success and challenge for both reading and language.

Along with daily reflections on independent reading, English learners should also have the opportunity to reflect on other independent work. Because they have many menu choices for guided learning experiences during the workshop time, it is important that they are able to set their own goals and/or objectives for their independent work. I find this goal setting, reflection, and sharing can help set students up for success during independent work time by giving them choice; it also encourages them to specifically focus on how they will spend their time. Additionally, this allows students to reflect on how their independent workshop time went. This reflection can also be used for accountability. English learners can share their goals with peers and check in at the end of the workshop with options for documentation to share with the teacher.

Date	Title/Author	Time/Pages	What went well? (one reading/one language)	What was a challenge? (one reading/one language)

Figure 7.1 *Adapted Reading Log*

This can be done orally or in writing in a log, a reader's response notebook, or a small sheet of paper they turn in, among other options.

Culminating Reflection and Sharing

As discussed in previous chapters, I recommend planning and working toward a culminating event or project. The project and sharing should incorporate the application of big ideas presented throughout the unit of study. I also see this as a time for English learners to celebrate their work and progress in meaningful ways as they share with peers, family, or other school community members. Too often English learners see instruction as a series of unconnected lessons with specific skills to be acquired and demonstrated for a test or some other evaluation measure. The goal of units of study is to connect language and literacy instruction in meaningful ways. For English learners, the consistency of theme and instruction provides background knowledge and vocabulary to support their development (Freeman and Freeman 2000). Building on this idea, it is helpful for students to see their work (whole group, small group, partner, and independent) reflected in an end project or goal. The culminating project should provide opportunities for integrating their learning related to language and reading in a summative way with a range of options depending on language proficiency.

◼ Specific Ideas for Instruction (Fiction and Informational Focus)

In the following sections, I include sample options for daily and culminating reflection and sharing. These samples include ideas for sharing and reflection with fiction and informational texts. In the daily sharing and reflection examples, modifications for differentiation are pretty straightforward and are addressed in the general chart for differentiation found in Chapter Two, so I don't include specific ideas again in this chapter. In the Culminating Project Rehearsal and Sharing section, I include ideas for differentiation according to stages of language proficiency and provide pictures of samples from classrooms ranging from kindergarten to fourth grade.

◼ Daily Sharing and Reflection Examples

There are many options for reflecting and sharing at the end of the workshop time. Revisiting and discussing the objectives or how it went, strategies students were using, and problems they encountered can support English learners in reflection. Here's a list of ways teachers can facilitate reflection and sharing with English learners:

- documenting and sharing from reader's response notebooks
- checklists of menu options during workshop time
- revisiting anchor charts with strategies and using physical representation or turn and talk to reflect on daily use
- turn and talk about how the workshop went in general
- sharing their favorite part of their reading
- sharing their successes from independent reading and work
- progress sharing with partners by showing or presenting their most recent progress during reading or toward culminating projects.

Including an emphasis on second language development with reflection helps English learners become metacognitive about both their reading and language processes. The more specific examples that follow include considerations for reflection and sharing about reading and language development.

Goals and Accomplishments Notebooks

I worked with a fifth-grade teacher who was teaching in English at an early exit bilingual school in a classroom of twenty-eight English learners. Her students wrote their goals and accomplishments in their reading response notebook every day. The English learners (all of the students in the class) would write down what they intended to accomplish during workshop with at least one literacy goal and one language goal. The literacy goals ranged from "reading twenty-five pages and completing my log" to "finding, documenting, and citing three new pieces of information for my research project on immigration." The language goals ranged from "learn and add two new terms to my personal glossary" to "write my three new pieces of information in past tense." Typically, the English learners were setting goals based on what they were working on during small groups or suggestions from conferring sessions with the teacher. After the goal setting and sharing with a peer, students began their independent work while the teacher met with small groups or facilitated conferring sessions.

At the end of workshop time, she gave them three minutes to jot down what they accomplished, rate themselves based on their goal, and write a note about where they would start and what they hoped to accomplish the following day. Typically, this became their goal for workshop time the following day, but she always gave them the option to change their goal before sharing it with partners and starting workshop. She checked in and responded to these goals one to two times a week when she was responding to their reading response notebooks. If she noticed a student needed extra support, she would check in on a daily basis and provide friendly reminders as needed.

Goal-Oriented To-Do List

I am a big advocate of modeling literate practices we find in the "real world." Because of this, I always try to model processes that work for me as a reader and writer. Although no one evaluates my setting and meeting of goals or tasks on a daily basis, I do make and modify a goal-oriented to-do list every day. I also have a writing partner with whom I exchange goals, deadlines, and writing on a weekly basis. A group of fourth graders (about half were English learners) laughed when I brought in my lists because I had long-term to-do lists, weekly to-do lists, project to-do lists, and daily to-do lists that were crossed out, erased, moved to another date. I recommend introducing the goal-oriented to-do list by showing students what you use. I started with a project (I was actually working on this book at the time of the lesson I was teaching to the fourth graders) and a list of all of the big ideas and major work that needed to be done. After sharing this with students, I related it to their culminating project of a research poster and presentation. I showed them my deadline and explained how I planned my work backward from that date. As a class, we made a mock schedule for the culminating project before students worked on their own schedule and to-do list. This gave us the big picture and general idea of what they wanted to accomplish while working toward the completion of the unit of study.

Based on our initial planning, we created a daily goal-oriented to-do list. I shared with them that I check in with my writing partner on a regular basis, and I told them they would be checking in with their partner using their goal-oriented to-do list for the culminating event. I requested they include one language "to-do" on their daily list. Some examples included the following: "read fifteen pages, write three "I learned" statements, use one new vocab"; "make a pictur [*sic*] and caption, read, find two words for glossary." Some days the students accomplished all of their tasks and had to move on to new work, but other days they only completed one or two items on their to-do list. This is perfectly normal—it happens to me on an almost daily basis!

Work with students to reflect on their progress and set goals for the following day. If students are not completing work as expected, problem solve with the student during a conferring session. This could include but is not limited to finding texts at an independent level, setting realistic goals, minimizing social conversations with peers, creating an environment conducive to that student's learning style, or additional strategy or language support from small-group or conferring sessions. For English learners, the language goals or to-do items sometimes prove to be more difficult to generate than content-based goals. I use conferring time to discuss and help set goals with English learners. A simple reminder of a focus or objective from small-group instruction can be a helpful way to establish how they will focus on and refine their language use in the authentic context of their culminating project.

■ Culminating Project/Event Sharing Examples

As mentioned previously, the culminating project and sharing should incorporate skills developed throughout the unit of study. Regardless of the unit focus, introduce the culminating event early on so English learners have an idea of what we will be working toward. By bringing together literacy and language learning, English learners have the opportunity to review and demonstrate their learning in a summative way. This should also be a time of celebration as the class celebrates its progress. This will look very different depending on the focus of the unit and the selected culminating project. For example, a unit on character development might have a culminating event of readers' theatre performances for peers, other classes, or parents. A unit of study on poetry, as suggested in Chapter Three, might have a culminating event of a "coffeehouse" performance where students perform selected poetry they have written to small groups in a coffeehouse or open mic–like setting. Figure 7.2 is a picture of first-grade English learners in Rachael Pritchard's class rehearsing for their poetry presentation.

Figure 7.2
Poetry Rehearsals

All of these culminating events allow English learners to demonstrate their knowledge using both expressive and receptive language by reading, writing, speaking, and listening. The following two examples of culminating events include ideas for an author unit of study and an inquiry research project unit of study.

Response Culmination, Celebration of Work, and Book Award (Fiction)

During the Kevin Henkes author unit mentioned in Chapter Five, I was teaching second grade in an English instruction classroom in a bilingual elementary school. Approximately 75 percent of my students' first language was Spanish, and I also had one student whose first language was Hmong. During this unit, we used a new reading response format (Figure 5.2) as a way to reflect on and document their understanding of and reaction to the text. Although this was a new and important way to respond to literature, I explained to the students that we would be completing responses to all the Kevin Henkes' books we read (most were read in small groups, pairs, or independently). At the end of the unit, we would nominate and select the class' favorite Kevin Henkes' book.

Students completed and kept their reading responses to the books (some students had five while others had as many as ten or more). Suggestions for differentiation for reading responses for English learners were addressed in Chapter Five. At the end of the unit, students compiled their reading responses, ranked them in order of favorite to least favorite. They had to select their favorite book and write down their supporting reason on a separate sheet of paper. For Beginning and Emerging English learners, I provided the language frame "My favorite Kevin Henkes' book was_____ because _____." I bound their best book selection reasoning page and reading responses in their ranked order with construction paper and a plastic binding to create their own book titled *Kevin Henkes Author Study: Reading Responses and Award Selection* by (student name).

Then, students met in four small groups to present their selection and reasoning and vote on the group's favorite selection. Within the small groups, students created a brief but persuasive presentation to share their favorite book with the class. All groups presented and the class voted (*Chrysanthemum* won). We read aloud *Chrysanthemum* as a part of our unit of study reflection. I emphasized that we were celebrating their hard work and study of Kevin Henkes and encouraged students to share their Kevin Henkes' book of reading responses and award designation with their family. For English learners, this allows multiple exposures to texts by the same author so they could build background knowledge on the style, characters, and themes. Additionally, the visual, written, and oral reading responses provide a scaffold to review previous reading material and discuss reasoning for their favorite book selection with peers. We were able to celebrate their progress with their award and author book that they could take home and share with their family.

Culminating Project Rehearsal and Sharing (Informational)

The inquiry research projects referenced in previous chapters all involve some type of independent inquiry from the English learners throughout the course of the unit. I find giving English learners choice in their research content/focus and choice in their representation increases motivation and enhances the final product. Another important aspect is providing an audience for their research and writing. They need to share their new learning with someone other than the teacher! For this to be successful, I recommend modeling, consistent conferring, and feedback throughout the independent inquiry process. I use the daily reflections and sharing to help guide this process, but conferring also plays a crucial role in supporting a large culminating project like a research poster, report, and/or presentation to peers or community members.

I did some team-teaching (in English) in a bilingual second-grade classroom to support a unit of study on informational text and the inquiry process. Each week I taught an anchor lesson to support the process. As the semester continued, the English learners documented their learning through illustrations with nonfiction text features, questions, "I learned" statements, and information they found interesting. The teachers commented that some of their students just kept collecting information, but they were uncertain about how to put it together in a cohesive format. I decided to model putting the poster together and practicing a presentation. I modeled the common challenges English learners face when first learning to present so students could be successful.

First, I asked students to help me put my research poster together. I took out all of the pieces I had been working on. This included questions, "I learned" statements, illustrations with captions and labels, and summaries. Students helped me decide where to place these on a large poster. Then, I suggested adding headings and a title to make the poster easier to read. Students helped me to construct my poster, and when I was finished, I told them I was going to present. I wanted them to give me suggestions for what would make my presentation better. I stood directly in front of the research poster with my back facing the students. They could see the back of my body and only part of the poster because I was blocking it. Then, I used a rapid and monotone voice and modeled stumbling over and getting stuck on some of the words I was reading.

At the completion of my presentation, I asked the students to respond to my presentation by asking a question, making a comment, and discussing some ideas that would make my presentation better. The presentation suggestions included the following: face the audience, slow down the pace, speak in a loud and clear voice with expression, practice your presentation so you are familiar with all the words, stand to the side of the poster, and periodically point to the portion of the poster you are discussing. I added these strategies to the research chart, and I suggested students start trying to use these strategies as they rehearsed their presentations. We gave them time to present their research posters during the middle and end stages of the project. We felt it was important to "try it out" and get feedback at the middle stage where the English learners could make changes, add information, organize, and reorganize their research posters and presentations without feeling defeated because they had to redo a large amount of work after they believed they were finished. They also presented and got feedback from the same small group prior to their final presentation that was done for their fifth-grade buddy.

Versions of this type of work with informational texts, inquiry, and presentations have been done in classrooms of many teachers I have the privilege of working with. Figure 7.3 is a picture of Rachel Busetti Frevert's second-grade English learners rehearsing their research poster presentation for a small group of peers. Figures 7.4 and 7.5 are pictures of Amy Fletcher's fourth graders (both English learners and monolingual English speakers) working together on the research posters prior to final presentations. Finally, Figure 7.6 is a picture of the culminating reef inquiry project from Beth Roger's diverse kindergarten class (with English learners, monolingual speakers, and students receiving regular and special education services). Her kindergarten students conducted independent inquiry projects on sea turtles, ocean animals, and habitats when they became concerned about the effects of pollution on reefs and animals. Moving beyond their original culminating project of independent inquiry posters, they made class posters discouraging polluting and designed an artificial reef. The reef in the picture is on permanent display at The Environmental Studies Center (a Florida Ecological and Educational Center in Martin County). What a perfect example of how purposeful research with an authentic audience can motivate English learners to engage with complex academic text and scientific concepts.

All of these teachers, with various age ranges, curriculum requirements, and student interests, managed to facilitate meaningful culminating projects where English learners took pride in their successful completion of research and presentation. Following are some ideas for differentiation for the culminating projects rehearsal and sharing we used with the second-grade English learners in the previous example.

Differentiation and Considerations According to Proficiency Levels

Stages of Language Proficiency	Teacher Roles	English Learner Expectations/Performance
STAGE 1: *Preproduction Silent Period (Starting)*	☐ Use slowed speech and emphasize vocabulary by pointing to, gesturing, and repeating essential words during the model lessons. ☐ When possible, pair with a classmate who speaks the student's first language. ☐ When conferencing with stage 1 students, focus on image with the possibility of a copied one- to two-word label.	☐ Could participate in partner research project with minimal input. ☐ Should be able to point to images. ☐ Can listen to teacher or partner read aloud. ☐ Can copy or create images. ☐ Can use first language to label or name images. ☐ May be able to copy image and brief label.

Figure 7.3
Research Poster Rehearsal

Figure 7.4
Research Poster Work

Stages of Language Proficiency *(continued)*	Teacher Roles	English Learner Expectations/Performance
STAGE 2: *Early Production (Emerging)*	☐ Encourage students to document understanding in first and second language when possible with labels and/or captions. ☐ Provide sentence starters for captions to share in presentation. Example: This is a picture of _____. ☐ When conferencing with stage 2 students, focus on images and simple copied labels. Scribe captions when possible and encourage rehearsal and sharing with peers.	☐ Can point to images, labels, and captions. ☐ Can copy or create images with simple labels. ☐ Can attempt to fill in the blank and/or copy the sentence starter. ☐ Can share simple labels or a brief copied or scribed caption with partners or small groups after having a chance to practice/rehearse.

(continues)

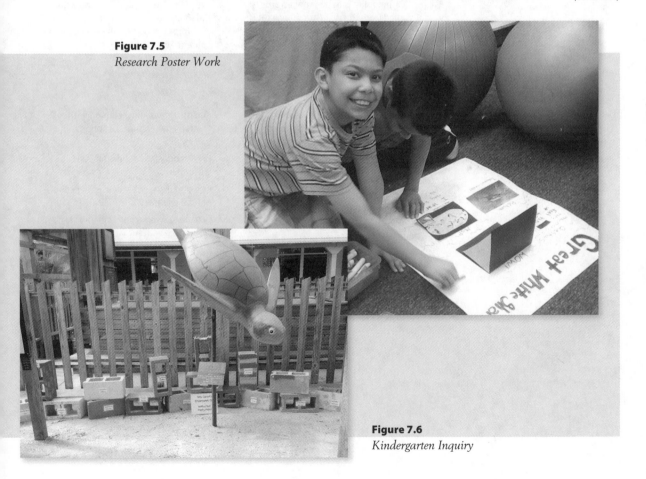

Figure 7.5
Research Poster Work

Figure 7.6
Kindergarten Inquiry

Stages of Language Proficiency (continued)	Teacher Roles	English Learner Expectations/Performance
STAGE 3: *Speech Emergence (Developing)*	☐ Encourage students to create an image and label (in English). ☐ Ask students to share their written caption using the sentence starter provided. ☐ Encourage students to share their writing with a partner before sharing with the small group or whole class.	☐ Can identify and replicate image, label, and caption (using sentence starter). ☐ Can share learning and image, label, and caption by reading off the poster with small or whole group after having a chance to practice/rehearse. ☐ Can use feedback to adjust their oral presentation.
STAGE 4: *Intermediate Fluency (Expanding)*	☐ Ask students to orally present their image with 2–5 labels. ☐ Ask students to present a caption from their learning that is in their own words, not copied from the text (summarize their learning). ☐ Encourage students to discuss and share with partners, small group, and whole class for feedback on poster and presentation skills.	☐ Can document new learning by creating an image with 2–5 labels and a self-created caption. ☐ Can share writing and thinking with classmates by reading from the poster and improvisational conversation about content when asked questions. ☐ Can use feedback to adjust their poster and oral presentation.
STAGE 5: *Advanced Fluency (Bridging)*	☐ Encourage students to move beyond initial instruction and modeling by providing the image, labels, and captions in their own words, identifying difficult vocabulary with accompanying explanations, and discussing possible consequences of natural disasters. ☐ Encourage students to create an oral presentation that does not include reading verbatim off their poster, but instead encourages the presentation of information learned and facilitation of a conversation about the topic.	☐ Can document new learning with self-created images, labels, captions, and summaries. ☐ Can identify and define difficult vocabulary. ☐ Can discuss possible consequences of natural disasters. ☐ Can share writing and thinking with classmates without direct reading from research poster. ☐ Can facilitate a conversation about the researched topic. ☐ Can use feedback to adjust their poster and oral presentation.

Reflection

☐ Consider your current opportunities for reflection and sharing. How frequently do they happen? In what ways might you be able to make this part of your daily and culminating routines during your units of study?

☐ What opportunities do you provide for your English learners to reflect on their literacy and content accomplishments? What opportunities do you provide for your English learners to reflect on their language growth and development?

☐ How might you integrate a goals and accomplishments notebook or a goal-oriented to-do list in an upcoming unit of study to support your English learners in reflecting and sharing their language and literacy progress?

☐ Consider your current culminating projects and sharing. How might you enhance them to offer authentic, real-world purposes and audiences for your English learners to utilize their language and literacy skills?

☐ How might you differentiate your daily and culminating reflection and sharing to meet the specific needs of the students in your classroom?

References

Allington, Richard L. 1991. "Children Who Find Learning to Read Difficult: School Responses to Diversity." In *Literacy for a Diverse Society: Perspectives, Practices, and Policies,* edited by Elfrieda H. Heiber, 237–52. New York: Teachers College Press.

———. 2000. *What Really Matters for Struggling Readers: Designing Research Based Programs.* Columbus, OH: Allyn & Bacon.

August, Diane, Maria Carlo, Cheryl Dressler, and Catherine Snow. 2005. "The Critical Role of Vocabulary Development for English Language Learners." *Learning Disabilities Research and Practice* 20 (1): 50–57.

Berman, Paul, Catherine Minicucci, Barry McLaughlin, Beryl Nelson, and Katrina Woodworth. 1995. *School Reform and Student Diversity: Case Studies of Exemplary Practices for LEP Students.* Washington, DC: National Clearinghouse for English Language Acquisition.

Bernhardt, Elizabeth B. 2011. *Understanding Advanced Second-Language Reading.* New York: Routledge.

Bradley, Lynette, and Peter E. Bryant. 1983. "Categorizing Sounds and Learning to Read: A Causal Connection." *Nature* 30: 419–21.

Buhrow, Brad, and Anne Upczak Garcia. 2006. *Ladybugs, Tornadoes, and Swirling Galaxies: English Learners Discover Their World Through Inquiry.* Portland, ME: Stenhouse.

Calkins, Lucy. 2001. *The Art of Teaching Reading.* New York: Addison-Wesley Longman.

———. 2010. *A Guide to the Reading Workshop.* Portsmouth, NH: Heinemann.

Calkins, Lucy, and Kathleen Tolan. 2010. *Building a Reading Life: Stamina Fluency, and Engagement*. Portsmouth, NH: Heinemann.

Carrison, Catherine, and Gisela Ernst-Slavit. 2005. "From Silence to a Whisper to Active Participation: Using Literature Circles with ELL Students." *Reading Horizons* 46 (2): 93–113.

Caswell, Linda J., and Nell K. Duke. 1998. "Non-Narrative as a Catalyst for Literacy Development." *Language Arts* 75 (2): 108–17.

Cohen, Dorothy. 1968. "The Effect of Literature on Vocabulary and Reading Achievement." *Elementary English* 45: 209–17.

Cummins, James. 1979. "Cognitive/Academic Language Proficiency, Linguistic Interdependence, the Optimum Age Question and Some Other Matters." *Working Papers on Bilingualism*, No. 19, 121–29.

———. 1991. "Interdependence of First- and Second-Language Proficiency in Bilingual Children." In *Language Processing in Bilingual Children*, edited by Ellen Bialystok, 70–89. Cambridge: Cambridge University Press.

———. 2003. "Reading and the Bilingual Student: Fact and Friction." In *English Learners: Reaching the Highest Level of English Literacy*, edited by Gilbert Garcia, 2–33. Newark, DE: International Reading Association.

———. 2008. "BICS and CALP: Empirical and Theoretical Status of the Distinction." In *Encyclopedia of Language and Education*, vol. 2, edited by Nancy Hornberger, 71–84. New York: Springer Science and Business Media.

Darling-Hammond, Linda. 1995. "Inequality and access to knowledge." In *Handbook of Research on Multicultural Education*, edited by James A. Banks and Cherry A. M. Banks, 465–83. New York: Macmillan.

Dickenson, David K., and Miriam W. Smith. 1994. "Long-Term Effects of Preschool Teachers' Book Readings on Low-Income Children's Vocabulary and Story Comprehension." *Reading Research Quarterly* 29:105–22.

Doherty, William R., Soleste H. Hilberg, America Pinal, and Roland G. Tharp. 2003. "Five Standards and Student Achievement." *NABE Journal of Research and Practice* 1: 1–24.

Drucker, Mary J. 2003. "What Reading Teachers Should Know About ESL Learners." *The Reading Teacher* 57: 22–29.

Echevarria, Jana, Deborah Short, and MaryEllen Vogt. 2008. *Making Content Comprehensible for English Learners: The SIOP Model*. Boston, MA: Pearson Education.

Freeman, David, and Yvonne Freeman. 2000. *Teaching Reading in Multilingual Classrooms*. Portsmouth, NH: Heinemann.

Gibbons, Pauline. 2002. *Scaffolding Language, Scaffolding Learning: Teaching Second Language Learners in the Mainstream Classroom*. Portsmouth, NH: Heinemann.

Harvey, Stephanie and Anne Goudvis. 2000. *Strategies that Work: Teaching Comprehension to Enhance Understanding*. Portland, ME: Stenhouse.

Guccione [Moses], Lindsey. 2010. An Ethnographic Approach to Examine the Community of Practice, Literacy Practices, and Construction of Meaning Among First-Grade Linguistically Diverse Learners. Doctoral dissertation. Available from Dissertations and Theses database at University of Northern Colorado (Publication No. AAT 3415987).

———. 2011. "Integrating Literacy and Inquiry for English Learners." *The Reading Teacher* 64 (8): 567–77.

Gutiérrez, Kris, and Marjorie F. Orellana. 2006. "The 'Problem' of English Learners: Constructing Genres of Difference." *Research in the Teaching of English* 40 (4): 502–07.

Gutiérrez, Kris, P. Zitlali Morales, and Danny C. Martinez. 2009. "Remediating Literacy: Culture, Difference, and Learning for Students from Non-Dominant Communities." *Review of Research in Education* 33: 212–45.

Hakuta, Kenji, and Maria Santos. 2012. "Understanding Language: Challenges and Opportunities for Language Learning in the Context of Common Core State Standards and Next Generation Science Standards." Stanford, CA: Stanford University. Accessed December 4, 2014. http://ell.stanford.edu/sites/default/files/Conference%20Summary_0.pdf.

Hakuta, Kenji, Yuko Goto Butler, and Daria Witt. 2000. *How Long Does It Take English Learners to Attain Proficiency?* Santa Barbara, CA: University of California, Linguistic Minority Research Institute.

Halladay, Juliet L. 2008. "Reconsidering Frustration-Level Texts: Second Graders' Experiences with Difficult Texts." Paper presented at the annual meeting of the National Reading Conference, December 4, Orlando, FL.

———. 2012. "Revisiting Key Assumptions of the Reading Level Framework." *The Reading Teacher* 66 (1): 53–62.

Hansen, Donald A. 1989. "Locating Learning: Second Language Gains and Language Use in Family, Peer and Classroom Contexts." *NABE The Journal for the National Association for Bilingual Education* 13 (2):161–80.

Helman, Lori, Donald R. Bear, Sharne Templeton, Marcia Invernizzi, and Francine Johnston. 2011. *Words Their Way with English Learners: Word Study for Phonics, Vocabulary, and Spelling*. Boston, MA: Pearson.

Herrera, Socorro G., Della R. Perez, and Kathy Escamilla. 2010. *Teaching Reading to English Language Learners: Differentiated Literacies.* Boston, MA: Pearson.

Hickman, Peggy, Sharolyn Pollard-Durodola, and Sharon Vaughn. 2004. "Storybook Reading: Improving Vocabulary and Comprehension for English-Language Learners." *The Reading Teacher* 57 (8): 720–30.

Kame'enui, Edward J., and Deborah C. Simmons. 2001. "Introduction to This Special Issue: The DNA of Reading." *Scientific Studies of Reading* 5 (3): 203–10.

Kindler, Anneka L. 2002. *Survey of the States' Limited English Proficient Students and Available Educational Programs and Services: 2000–2001 Summary Report.* Washington, DC: National Clearinghouse for English Language Acquisition.

Krashen, Stephen D. 1987. *Principles and Practice in Second Language Acquisition.* Englewood Cliffs, NJ: Prentice-Hall.

Krashen, Stephen D., and Tracy Terrell. 1983. *The Natural Approach: Language Acquisition in the Classroom.* Oxford: Pergamon.

Kendal, Julie, and Outey Khuon. 2005. *Making Sense: Small-Group Comprehension Lessons for English Language Learners.* Portland, ME: Stenhouse Publishers.

MacSwan, Jeff, Kellie Rolstad, and Gene V. Glass. 2002. "Do Some School-Age Children Have No Language? Some Problems of Construct Validity in the Pre-LAS Espanol." *Bilingual Research Journal* 26 (2): 213–38.

Migdol, Robin. 2011. *Stanford Researcher Launches National K–12 English Language Learning Initiative.* Stanford Report, accessed July 1, 2014. http://news.stanford.edu.

Montecel, Maria R., and Josie D. Cortez. 2002. "Successful Bilingual Education Programs: Development and the Dissemination of Criteria to Identify Promising and Exemplary Practices in Bilingual Education at the National Level." *Bilingual Research Journal* 26: 1–22.

Muter, Valerie, Charles Hulme, Margaret J. Snowling, and Jim Stevenson. 2004. "Phonemes, rimes, vocabulary, and grammatical skills as foundations of early reading development: evidence from a longitudinal study." *Developmental Psychology* 40: 663–81.

National Assessment of Educational Progress. 2009. *The Nation's Report Card: Reading Grade 4 National Results.* Washington, DC: Author.

National Governors Association Center for Best Practices and Council of Chief State School Officers. 2010a. *Application of Common Core State Standards for English Language Learners.* Washington, DC: Author. Accessed May 5, 2014. www.core standards.org/assets/application-for-english-learners.pdf.

———. 2010b. *Common Core State Standards for English Language Arts & Literacy in History/Social Studies, Science, and Technical Subjects.* Washington, DC: Author.

National Research Council. 1997. *Improving Schooling for Language-Minority Children*. Washington, DC: National Academies Press.

Office of English Language Acquisition, Language Enhancement and Academic Achievement for Limited English Proficient Students. 2010. *The Growing Number of English Learner Students 1997/1998–2007/2008*. Washington, DC: U.S. Department of Education.

Opitz, Michael F., and Lindsey Moses Guccione. 2009. *Comprehension and English Language Learners: 25 Oral Reading Strategies That Cross Proficiency Levels*. Portsmouth, NH: Heinemann.

Opitz, Michael F., and Michael P. Ford. 2001. *Reading Readers: Flexible and Innovative Strategies for Guided Reading*. Portsmouth, NH: Heinemann.

———. 2008. *Doable Differentiation: Varying Groups, Texts and Supports to Reach Readers*. Portsmouth, NH: Heinemann.

Orellana, Maria, and Kris Gutiérrez. 2006. "What's the Problem? Constructing Different Genres for the Study of English Learners." *Research in the Teaching of English* 41 (1): 118–23.

Pappas, Christine C. 1991. "Fostering Full Access to Literacy by Including Information Books." *Language Arts* 68 (6): 449–62.

Pearson, P. David, and Margaret C. Gallagher. 1983. "The Instruction of Reading Comprehension." *Contemporary Educational Psychology* 8: 317–44.

Purcell-Gates, Victoria, Nell K. Duke, and Joseph A. Martineau. 2007. "Learning to Read and Write Genre Specific Text: Roles of Authentic Experience and Explicit Teaching." *Reading Research Quarterly* 42 (1): 8–45.

Ramirez, David J. 1992. "Longitudinal Study of Structured English Immersion Strategy, Early-Exit and Late-Exit Transitional Bilingual Education Program for Language-Minority Children." *Bilingual Research Journal* 16: 1–62.

Ray, Katie Wood. 2006. *Study Driven: A Framework for Planning Units of Study in the Writing Workshop*. Portsmouth, NH: Heinemann.

Ruiz-de-Velasco, Jorge, and Michael Fix. 2000. *Overlooked and Underserved: Immigrant Students in U.S. Secondary Schools*. The Urban Institute Report. Washington, DC: The Urban Institute.

Serafini, Frank. 2001. *The Reading Workshop: Creating Space for Readers*. Portsmouth, NH. Heinemann.

———. 2012. "What Are We Differentiating in Differentiated Instruction?" *Journal of the Reading Association of Ireland* (Fall): 12–16.

Serafini, Frank, with Suzette Serafini-Youngs. 2006. *Around the Reading Workshop in 180 Days: A Month-by-Month Guide to Effective Instruction*. Portsmouth, NH: Heinemann.

Serravallo, Jennifer. 2010. *Teaching Reading in Small Groups: Differentiated Instruction for Building Strategic, Independent Readers.* Portsmouth, NH: Heinemann.

Serravallo, Jennifer, and Gravity Goldberg. 2007. *Conferring with Readers: Supporting Each Student's Growth and Independence.* Portsmouth, NH: Heinemann.

Taberski, Sharon. 2000. *On Solid Ground: Strategies for Teaching Reading K–3.* Portsmouth, NH: Heinemann.

TESOL. 2006. *Prek–12 English Language Proficiency Standards.* www.tesol.org/docs /books/bk_prek-12elpstandards_framework_318.pdf?sfvrsn=2.

Tomlinson, Carol A. 2001. *How to Differentiate Instruction in Mixed-Ability Classrooms.* Alexandria, VA: Association for Supervision and Curriculum Development.

Ulanoff, Sharon H., and Sandra L. Pucci. 1999. "Learning Words from Books: The Effects of Read-Aloud on Second Language Vocabulary Acquisition." *Bilingual Research Journal* (23): 409–22.

Valdés, Guadalupe, George C. Bunch, Catherine Snow, Carol Lee, and Lucy Matos. 2005. "Enhancing the Development of Students' Language(s): An Introduction for Teachers." In *Preparing Teachers for a Changing World: What Teachers Should Learn and Be Able to Do*, edited by Linda Darling-Hammond, John Bransford, Pamela LePage, Karen Hammerness, and Helen Duffy, 126–67. National Academy of Education. San Francisco: Jossey Bass.

Vygotsky, Lev. 1978. *Mind in Society.* Cambridge, MA: Harvard University Press.

Wells, Gordon. 1999. *Dialogic Inquiry: Towards a Sociocultural Practice and Theory of Education.* Cambridge, United Kingdom: Cambridge University Press.